Drawn In Dust

*To Dave & Jan,
Florida friends
who have made my
stay interesting —
and worth the trip!*

Jane Mayes
3/9/15

Poems of life by

Jane Mayes

authorHOUSE®

AuthorHouse™
1663 Liberty Drive
Bloomington, IN 47403
www.authorhouse.com
Phone: 1-800-839-8640

© 2011 Jane Mayes. All rights reserved.

No part of this book may be reproduced, stored in a retrieval system, or transmitted by any means without the written permission of the author.

First published by AuthorHouse   4/21/2011

ISBN: 978-1-4520-9981-1 (sc)
ISBN: 978-1-4520-9980-4 (hc)
ISBN: 978-1-4520-9982-8 (e)

Library of Congress Control Number: 2010919565

Printed in the United States of America

This book is printed on acid-free paper.

Because of the dynamic nature of the Internet, any Web addresses or links contained in this book may have changed since publication and may no longer be valid. The views expressed in this work are solely those of the author and do not necessarily reflect the views of the publisher, and the publisher hereby disclaims any responsibility for them.

Cover design and illustrations by Donald Bullis

This book is dedicated to:

Ed, who devoted his life to me, grounded me, yet gave me
    freedom to fly.
Carrie, Jill and Jon, who began as our children
    and evolved into my friends.
Paul and Teresa, my admired and appreciated
    son- and daughter-in-loves.
Lucy, Eddie, Maxine, Haley, Henry and Ellen,
    grandchildren who warm my heart and light my life.
Hub, my editor-father, who revered the printed word and never
    let a typo get past him.
Julia, my mother, who was the best teacher I ever had.
Don, who shares his love of art, music and writing with me.
My friends and relatives who have raised my spirits in times
    of crises and celebrated the good times.
You, the reader who has been drawn to read these poems.

Bless you all!

Acknowledgments

I wish to thank Mary Brown and Judy Beam for the many hours they devoted to critique and edit the manuscript during its preparation; Don Bullis, who produced the art work; my niece Jennifer Clark, poet and encourager; Patty Finan for her computer expertise; Betty Bond for her counsel; Enid Maxwell, now deceased, who started all this when she asked the question years ago, "Why don't you put your poems in a book?"; Chris Clancy, Ann Schwedler (now dec.) and Mary, who were three-fourths of the PMs (Post-Manuscript) poetry support group; the Bards of Bird Creek; neighbors in our village; and strangers who provided fodder for my imagination.

Table of Contents

Dedication & Acknowledgments	vii
Beginnings	1
Family	21
Friends	61
Neighbors	99
Relationships	129
Love	177
Loss	227
Recovery	261

Drawn in Dust

Our lives are sketches drawn in the dust of time—
vignettes that capture the commonplace:
    spent tea cups on the patio,
    children's laughter echoing,
    a glass of cool water,
    foals bucking in the meadow,
    handprints on a window pane,
    cracker crumbs by a favorite chair,
    boots caked with mud,
    sand burrs on ragg socks.

It's the homely things after all
    that are the meat of living,
    that become so precious
    just before they're blown away
    by the winds of life passing.

Beginnings

In Utero

Dear little zygote
(now a cluster of cells),
you are almost nothing,
yet you are more
precious than platinum.
You have no memory
of your days-old past,
but in your being
lies the future
of your family.
Featureless now,
you will bear
the composite face
of ancestors unremembered.
It is good for you
to stay sequestered
until you develop
and we adjust, else,
in our delight
we might smother you
with our love.

No ZPG

We need babies

(babies in buntings,
babies in cribs,
babies in high chairs
drooling on bibs,
babies in playpens,
babes on the floor;
how many are there?
we need a few more!
crawling on laps,
swinging in swings)

to give hope for whatever
the future brings.

From Heaven To Heaven

Sweet child,
when I hold you near my heart
as you twizzle the hair
at the nape of my neck
before melting into sleep on my shoulder,

it's then I get a glimpse
of the comfort and bliss of heaven.

Missing Pages

Have I betrayed you, my daughter?
You so wanted to be pregnant,
and now in your second month you ask
between green-gilled waves of nausea,
"Is it worth it?"
I tell you the truth:
"You were worth it,
would be worth anything
I could go through."

Later will you curse me
for what I didn't tell:
that childbirth for me
was pelvis-splitting,
agonizing, self-exploding,
awe-filled pain
that only a human life
could be worth?

Will you forgive me, daughter?

Now as I already cherish
the growing life within you
as my own, I dread
what lies ahead for you
and tell myself that you
will birth more easily than I,
that I am just a weakling
with a low pain tolerance.

Oh, daughter, don't hate me
for the chapter I left out.

Identity

Who are you, Lucy?
We don't know you yet.
You haven't told us;
but just before you smile
your eyes twinkle
like great-grampa's
under your daddy's eyebrows.
You listen to a distant sound
through his finely-sculpted ears
beside Grandma Grippo's face.

Your mother's hands,
borrowed from your matronym,
assume a ballet pose
as you relax in sleep;
and angelic eyelashes
softly rest upon your cheeks.

Uncle Jon's inner contentment
and Grampa Mayes' curiosity
are already imprinted; and
your legs and arms are driven
by Aunt Carrie's passion
for activity.

But I see you and no one else
as you wrinkle your squinchy nose
before you break into a smile
and make the sun shine.

For Maxine

Before you were
I loved the possibility of your being.
    Then you became,
and I marveled at your protoplasmic potential;
but your first photo at birth-minus-seven months
captivated this almost-grandmother's heart.
    As I viewed your budding form in awe,
I saw secrets unknown to previous generations.
    Yet gradually grandmothers adjust--
That's why you never read in the papers
about spontaneous heart combustion.

Ah! The Children

Cherish the children.
Listen to their babble
as if they were giving
directions to heaven.

Memorize their eager faces;
store up their happy laughter
as a substitute for sunrise
on gray mornings.

Remember the imprint
of their hand in yours
as they lead you
to limitless love.

Hold in your heart
their hope for a world
that heals its scars
with the balm of peace.

Artistic Limitations

Who can paint the wonder
    that is a toddler?

Silken skin brushed
    by fluttering angel wings,
cheeks the color of
    pink rose petals,
eyes that reflect multitudes
    of marvels in a world
    completely new,
hair that's down,
    then flying up before
    the brush can make its stroke,
hands that tug, and arms
    that hug spontaneously.

What pigment do you use
    to depict pristine purity
    yet unblemished by the world?
And how do you capture
    boundless enthusiasm,
    bounding energy,
and contain the flow of questions
    on the canvas?

Poem in Lieu of Praise

"Words! Words!

    Words float around in the air!

    MONEY you can hold in your pocket!" *

So don't THANK me,

    PAY me;

and I'll take the money and sock it.

Or, better yet,

    I'll SPEND it

on a record, book, or locket;

and when it's all gone,

I'll take something I bought,

    and go right out and hock it!

*Jill, age 5

Our Children

Fresh, unique…
something of their father,
something like their mother,
yet not a combination,
but a new creation
with new interests, new ideas,
thinking their own thoughts,
seeing the world differently,
following their own stars,
charting new courses,
planting their flags
on challenging mountains,
slaying different dragons.

Our children—
fresh, unique.

Birthday Poem

Should I design a card for thee,

it would surely show a tree

standing green and straight and tall

over heads and shoulders all,

with needles softened by compassion,

seeds within the cones all fashioned

by love and goodness – ready to grow

when planted by the son we know.

Saints Alive!

Did the baby Jesus squirm and wriggle,
play a prank on patient Joseph,
dimples denting, hide and seek,
tug at Mary's veil, then giggle?

I like to think that he was normal
for a boy of flesh and form.
If intellect sires sense of humor,
why are icons all so formal?

A statue with that vapid stare
and ever-somber piety
mirrors more the artist's nature
than that of child caught unaware.

Just for a realistic style
I'd like to see religious art
project a hint of happy heaven,
with at least an upturned smile.

Remember?

I don't remember...
being on that heavenly cloud
where babies wait to be conceived,
or when, where, or how it happened;
although I figured it out much later—

or rocking in that placental sea
for nine months while I waited to be born.
I don't remember my birth, either—
ejected against my will as
I struggled, gasping for air.
It must have been stressful
because I screamed like all get-out.
I only know these things because
Mother told me that my fingernails were long,
and I had beautiful, dainty ears.
I remember how she would fondle them
to get me to sleep as I grew a bit older,
and it worked mesmerizingly well.

I do remember being four
and teaching myself to read from a book
I'd place on the enameled pull-out counter
of the roll-top Sessions cabinet
as Mother rolled out pie crust
and I rolled words off my tongue.

To this day I relish the taste
of pie crust...
and words.

I Remember

I remember the metallic music
of the wheels of my clip-on skates
as they bore me to my favorite haven
those idyllic summers in the mid-1940's,
when time seemed to be a still-life painting.
As I remember, peace seeps into the cracks
of my harried, adult life.

The hard metal of the octagonal tip
of the skate key suspended from my neck
by an orphaned shoelace from
my brother's hightop tennies,
taps against my chest to match
the rhythm of my heart's throb.

I pass old Cora Wheeler's precise yard,
hoping the music they make won't
provoke another neighborly complaint.
My skate song seems minor compared to
the snake-steaks-in-a-bag gift from my brothers,
but you never know with Ms. Cora Wheeler.
Today, I wonder how the neighborhood youth
perceive my own scrutiny.

I'm gaining speed as I hop the curb
and round the corner past the home-office
of benevolent Dr. Pinkham, G.P.
who made a house call the day
my trike tipped and my chin skin ripped,
necessitating suturing on our dining table.

(cont.)

Now the wheels shush, shush, shush,
as they try to calm me before my arrival
at the Temple-of-All-Things-Good.
I slip my key off, release my skates,
and ascend the imposing marble steps
of this hallowed shrine.

The building is an impressive monument
to Alvah N. Belding, town benefactor.
Its imposing façade consumes the view
of the sluggish Flat River.
Grasping the gleaming brass handle
of the nine-foot, windowed door,
I feel an odd mixture of peace and excitement
as I pad silently over the shiny, rubbery floor
to return the book borrowed the previous day.
Although still eight, I bypass the children's section,
and turn right, into the young adult area.
Like a kid eyeing candy cases,
or a lion on the prowl, I sidle slowly past shelves,
savor titles, peruse favorite authors,
test-scan frontispieces for mood and
degree of fascination potential.
Ah! I invite Gene Stratton Porter to join me
on the window seat beneath its high-domed panes,
and take a test-read. This is it!

I shyly present my choice at the circulation desk,
where the crippled lady with glasses-on-a-chain
checks me out as she tells me why she likes this book.
Heart quickening, the shush-shushes sing faster now
as I cradle the precious loan and speed home.

Lying snugly on the couch,
book propped against my knee-mountain,
I become...the Girl of the Limberlost.

Sky-Swimming

"...He soared on the wings of the wind."
                              -Psalm 18:10

When I was a child
I flew on my own,
like a swimmer in the sky:

With a leap I'd ascend,
and soon I would be
clearing wires and buildings high.

Looking down, I could see
tall trees beneath me;
and friends would look up and say,

"There she goes, that girl;
she's at it again,"
and they'd go back to their play.

The earth couldn't hold
all the dreams in my brain,
so the sky was the only limit;

and when I'd start to fall,
I'd give it my all,
and once again I'd air-swim it.

It was such a let-down
to come back to earth,
and I'd settle down with a sigh.

Now that I'm grown
I haven't much flown,
but I know even now I *could* fly!

Growing Pains

It's been some time since, along the street
I've slowed my step for smaller feet
and felt a tiny hand in mine—
one which needed my touch, an outward sign
of strength, approval, a smiley face
of love no matter what the pace.

Though I still get a smile and a stolen hug or two,
now grown, the kids don't seem to need them;
but, oh, I know I do!

The Stork Has Landed

Oh, beautiful dream stork,
your sterile sword-beak
rests upon my shoulder
as if to dub me "Sir Mother"
before I put you behind me
and go on to another life.

Where is the fourth child
I awaited so long in vain?
I have seen her in Haiti,
Guatemala, in a travelogue,
Kosovo, on the evening news,
imagined him in a misty lineup
wearily waiting to be born.

Now in my age of reflection
and after all these years in labor,
am I to finally deliver
this child named Poetry?

Angst

In the middle of the darkest night
I am awakened by a scream.
It is my heart echoing
the collective angst
of children, mistreated,
tortured, sold, neglected.
Their tears run down my cheeks
as they huddle silently in dark corners,
weeping with me, awaiting rescue,
respite from their hopeless pain.

Oh, God, I pray;
send someone to love them,
a comforting, rescuing angel.

                        Send me.

Family

Regarding the Past

"Your history is so *new*,"
a European visitor commented
with curious smile,
    implying historic superiority,
not realizing that his twelfth-century castle
is ours as well,
and that the history of the world
is not *his* story, but *our* story—
    the biography of our human family.

Entering the museum
we are plunged into the struggles and styles
    of life in the 1800's.
Reliving those yesteryears spent
in the barns, fields and kitchens, we realize
    how limited were choices
    in food, clothing and travel,
how difficult the work
    and sparse the entertainment,
how uncomplicated the education of the young,
how neighbors joined in mutual struggle
    to raise a barn,
    race the weather to harvest,
    and save strangers from a sinking ship.

For many, our struggles today
are physically less taxing,
    but no less stressful;
yet who would say they'd willingly
    return to "the good old days";
for many here would have expired
    before their present age
without the medical advances
    of the intervening years.

In visiting the past
we gain appreciation for the present
and hope and courage to face the future
as we begin to write the next chapter
in the biography of humanity.

Quiltscape

Lying on the landscape
of Great Grandma's quilt
is like a magic carpet ride
back to Grandma's childhood.

Finger the wool serge
of her winter school dress
handed down sister-to-sister,
skirts barely revealing
the high button shoes
skipping down the long farm lane,
her gloved hand swinging
the tin lunch bucket
stuffed with thick bread
spread with freshly churned butter
and nestling home-cured bacon.

Fondle the lush, maroon velvet,
a Sunday-best dress. Picture
skirts protectively gathered
as she mounted the wagon
for the dusty ride to
the Klacking Creek Church.

Somber colors reflect
the unsmiling poses
of the sepia tintypes
in the family album.
Here Albert's rough coat,
there Theodore's pants,
(Grampa's suit in a previous life)
little Julia's pinafore,

Aunt Mary's cape, a summer blouse
worn for work around the house,
William's worsted shirt,
Valentine's vest, and
Barbara's home-spun skirt.

No closets were needed,
just three hooks.
An old Sunday-best
was handed down
or went to school, and
finally became field wear
before its final rest
in the earth of this quiltscape.

The random pattern recalled
the valley fields and woods
viewed from the top
of the creaky windmill—
fields of flannel and worsted,
striped, plaid, and patterned,
hound's tooth and fleur-de-lis
connected by an infinite pattern
of embroidery stitches that
fenced off the patches
as far as the horizon;

and hardly noticeable
at the bottom corner,
simply signed in floss:

Anna* March*
1909*

Vagaries of Chance

If great-grandma hadn't decided
    to cross the ocean on that boat,
and grandpa hadn't been a tinker,
    but wore a different coat;
if my mother had decided to turn another page,
and father had opted for life on the silver stage;
if your grandfather had up and quit the farm,
    and your grandma had headed
        for other climates warm;
if the circus had lured your father away,
and your mother had chosen another role to play,
could I be you,
    and you be me?
And where do you think that we would be?

Twiddling

Serenely she sits
in her rocking chair
as her granddaughter brushes
her long, grey hair and asks,

"Gramma, why do you twiddle
your thumbs like that?
Are you exercising them
so they won't get fat?"

Smiling gently, Gramma replies
with a hint of a twinkle
in her eyes, "It's just
a little game they play;
and when they get bored,
they go the other way!"

The Ghost in the Basement

After her death
my dreams told me where Gramma was:
down in the black hole that led under the kitchen—
a hole I had never dared to explore,
like the equally ominous coal bin.
I might have shone the fright away
with my flashlight once and for all,
but the idea of even that was taboo
for the cobweb-delicate mind of a nine-year-old.
Still, I didn't search for her there—
just knew the ghost was keeping her
and knew that's where she was,
like you know in dreams. I knew because
she would never go as far away
from me as heaven. At least this way
she was still that near—as near as fear;
and even tingling fear was a comfort
compared to the finality of death.
So in my dreams and in my longing
I opened the door at the top of the stair,
just a peek at first, for a glimpse of her jailer;
then to the top of the landing to peer into darkness
for a glance at its grayness disappearing into the hole.
In my loss I befriended fear, that shadowy specter,
meeting it half way, at the bottom of the steps,
where love and longing led to boldness,
and a deal was struck:
the ghost would let Gramma out of the black hole
to rock in her chair, hands folded in her lap,
on the edge of the Michigan cellar,
where I could sit at her feet
and be comforted by her presence.

The ghost led me through the cloud of fear
until I no longer needed the dream
once I realized that Gramma would never be
farther away than my heart,
which speeds its beat when I'm afraid,
reminding me that she is still with me.

What's a Mother To Do?

fix breakfast
rich smell of coffee
beckoning up the open stair
a molecular alarm clock
intruding upon dreams
of flying over the electric lines
get daddy off to the linotype
give us this day our daily pie
a cake will last two
dinner at noon, clean up
see if you can get everything done in the afternoon
but it never works that way

do the washing
sometimes all day monday
lucky you have an electric wringer
it makes life much easier
hang the clothes outdoors

ironing tuesday
(repeat stanza #1 above)

wednesday special projects
spackle the worn toilet room linoleum
paper the hall wall
sew up a dress for daughter
(when gramma spent the winter
you got off darning and mending)
paint a cupboard, make drapes
wash and stretch curtains
spade the garden
shovel the walk
(save daddy's heart so
he could outlive you by
a lonely eight years)

thursday do-gooding
visit a shut-in
clean the church basement
clerk the rummage sale
sew altar cloths for the missions

friday scrub the floor
dust the stairs down, never up
fresh doilies
dust the cellophane on the lampshades
and candles in their holders
(some day special we may light them)
we break for Mother of Perpetual Help devotions

saturday smell of fresh bread and
doughnuts smoking bubbly in the grease
kids get some holes rolled in sugar
bake extra for the weekend
you never know who may stop by
wash our hair with pine tar soap
confess your sins
your lustful longings for laziness
weekly bedtime baths

sunday Mass serve the Lord
and serve our dinner
after dishes your reward
an hour of classical music on the radio
with apples and popcorn and your feet up
before you made us supper
you finally sat down
to read the paper and fell asleep
with it spread out in your lap

good-night
God bless you and
don't forget your night prayers

New Tricks

Peering through the lace curtains
of the dining room
overlooking the two-path driveway
beside our house,
we witness the third day
of mother's bicycle-riding lessons
self-taught.

Movie camera ready,
we document the process,
giggling in disbelief:
    the mount,
    the takeoff,
    the half-pedal,
    the loss of balance,
    the landing
on the soft grass
between the tracks.
Maximum trip:
    ten feet.

"Forty-eight is too late."
She never learned,
but only quit trying
when she knew we were laughing.
Yet we were proud
that she tried.

My Hero

Here I sit cross-legged
on the window seat,
my Mary Jane shoes covered
tent-like by my dress.
I am like a dog that senses
when the children will return from school,
only this is more exciting.
I will see him when he turns the corner
two doors down the street.
Yes! There he comes!

I know he is happy—
absentmindedly whistling
his happy tune,
"Marching Through Georgia."
Soon Daddy swoops me up,
my Buster Brown haircut flying up
as I come back down to earth
giggling.

After our noon dinner
he kisses my mother on the cheek
and eases into his chair,
the foot of his crossed leg
almost touching the floor;
and I hop onto his ankle
for an after-dinner horsey ride.
As he reads the <u>Grand Rapids Press</u>,
I play with my box "desk"
behind his chair,
filing the sample forms
he has brought me
from his newspaper office.

(cont.)

A smoke signal
from his walking-to-work cigar
sends me skipping to his side.

We walk to the corner,
my tiny hand enveloped by his;
and looking way up
I see that smile
and the twinkle in his eye
that says we share a secret—
a secret we never had to tell each other,
we just knew.

Summer 1941

Contented mourning doves
coo-coo-coo-OOO-ooo
a casual invitation
to get up...or not,
maybe to laze a bit longer,
plan a pleasant summer day
or connect mental images
to the sounds rising
through the kitchen ceiling
with the scented coffee sprites.

Gray dobbin pauses patiently
before our house, limp-reined
as the milkman leaves
our clinking bottles at the door
before some invisible mind-signal
sets her clop-clopping on
to the next customer.

Now the tzz-z-z-z-z-z-z
wireless warning of the tree toads
completes the morning's alarm
along with the revived tar fumes
sun-simmering on the porch roof
outside the open bedroom door
as the heat piles up in bulging,
invisible bags of BTU's.

Wander out and chalk-mark
hopscotch squares on the sidewalk
under the maple leaf parasols.
Toss the flattened stone, then
hop-turn-stoop-pick-hop and toss again
until a "witch's darning needle"
hovers menacingly near

(cont.)

sending us home screaming
lest it sew our lips shut.

Later, slip on the shoestring necklace
with the skate-key pendant
and dance to the rhythm
of the noisy metal wheels
s-s-sh-h-h, s-s-sh-h-h
s-sh-ussh-ing each other in turn.
Skip over the sidewalk cracks
and hop the curbs until
you stand at the base of
The Monument to Imagination.

Ascend the multi-stepped entrance.
Leave your noisy skates
at the portals and enter
the hushed Temple of Words.
The smell of the waxed, rubbery floor,
like incense, can make you giddy
with anticipation.

Scan the tantalizing shelves
lined with undiscovered delights.
Select a well-used book,
checking the frontispiece
for the requisite promise of
adventure, intrigue and atmosphere.
Cozy up in the cushioned nook
below a high-domed window
for a test-read.

Skate-slide home clutching treasures
to savor in the cool shade
behind the hornpipe vine.
Disappear so far into the pages
that it takes six calls
to summon you back
to set the table for supper.

Fresh Apple-Popcorn Days

Ah, the crack
of the fresh Spy apple
as it split, revealing
the pattern of the womb
encircling embryonic fruit!

Popcorn kernels
hammered the lid
of the popper
in an enthusiastic, individualistic
effort to escape
(had they organized
and all popped at once,
they could have blown
the lid off).

The scent of the salty
butter esters released
by the heat of the popcorn
was heady incense that,
mixed with the music
of the radio Texaco Hour,
elevated us above the mundane.
The tartness of the fruit
with the buttery saltiness
created a taste ecstasy
best appreciated with closed eyes.

As we sat listening, munching,
thoughts were free to dream,
to roam the universe
with the orchestra
now leading us into battle,
cannons roaring,
sabers flashing,
now settling us
under a tree
near a sleepy meadow
of grazing cattle,
now dancing with us
in flowing formal attire
in a mirrored ballroom.

Apple-popcorn memories
add zest and warmth
to my days even now.

Sometimes Subterfuge

When I was just a toddler
and caught in childish lie,
my father punished me, to teach
that truth was always best;
and cover-up would always be
more difficult than honesty.
And staunchly I spent fifty years
of living by that code.

And then one day he greeted me
with welcome smile upon his face;
and, after chatting for a bit,
with some concern he looked about
and asked where Mother was,
his bride of sixty years ago,
adding that he hadn't seen her
    for a week or more.

"Oh, Dad," I then updated him,
"Don't you remember mother's death
three years ago after the fall
that broke her hip and kept her
in the nursing home a year?"

His eyes spilled tears of grief
as if he'd heard the news
    the first time, unprepared.
We wept together,
he in sorrow for his loss,
and I for having opened such a wound
where I'd intended to inject
    a healing dose of truth.

That's the day he taught me late
    the rule about exceptions—
sometimes subterfuge is best;
there's virtue in discretion
and kindness in the telling
    of a straight-out, loving lie.

The Brass Bed

After the funeral
we went to get the old brass bed,
my daughter and I
staying overnight
for an early morning start.
As we slept in it together,
like Pandora's box it loosed
from its springs
a store of memories
pent up for three generations.

Ghosts of separate pasts
joined us in that bed.
I, the older, knew
the bed recalled
my parents' wedding night.
And if that weren't enough,
it was the silent witness
of my own conception.
So it didn't seem
unusual at that time
to also serve as birthing bed
for all four offspring.

Toddlers frightened in the night
could clamber over the foot rail
and seek warm protection
between sleepy parents
where monsters couldn't reach.
When we had a fever,
it coddled us there
in the downstairs bedroom
near mother's watchful eye.
I in turn saw my mother lie here
for weeks after surgery.

Echoes of intimacy floated by,
muffled pillow talk
and light, delightful laughter
behind the closed bedroom door,
intriguing to a child
come downstairs
for a late-night drink of water.

My daughter had her own
memories to tell of visits
to Grampa and Gramma's,
of climbing over the foot rail,
and the smooth, cool feeling
of the flying-saucer posts,
and reading under
the fabric-covered light
that hung from the head rail.

The old bed had gone with Grampa
to his other daughter's house--
a comforting touch of home
in his final aloneness.

When she set it up
in her new house,
my daughter thought
she heard a sigh.

Collections

The spinster dowager aunt
has outlived them all.
She sits amid her treasures
and sorts broken costume jewelry
from a cigar box containing
four playing cards,
several scrabble squares,
a stapler, two safety pins,
a swizzle stick from the Ponchetrain,
two silver cocktail forks
and a rubber band-bound
packet of peel-off labels
that say, "HELLO! My name is:"

Dust collects on the china
service for almost twenty,
reminder of elaborate theme dinners
planned in detail by the frail one
to be carried out by
her willing sister-slave.

An open drawer reveals
"string too short to use,"
crinkled paper party favors
and mute noisemakers
which echo the cackling laughter
of ninety New Years' babies
grown old and bent and flimsy-haired.

Decaying designer dresses stuff closets
along with stiffening shoes,
arthritic alligator purses
and furs whose pelts have separated
but have not yet divorced.

In the attic, cobweb spirits hover,
hoping to be called up for action
that never materializes.
Surreal candles melt to
embrace old batteries
as if trying to re-energize
the brilliance of better days;
and faded feather centerpieces
lie dismantled by an itinerant mouse.

In the damp basement
moldy ghosts attach
to the fabric of a better day.
There lie frayed baskets
that held the happiness
of gathering bleached driftwood
to warm the hearth
where ashes now lie cold.

From his frame, Chopin
eyes shelves of partial sets
of classics whose print
has shrunk too small to read.
Behind the chilly furnace
tipsy empty vintage bottles
toast the dowager's decline.

Now-useless items
are crammed into the dumpster
of a formerly brilliant mind
clouded with the clutter
of too many memories saved
from a past that foretold so much.

Angel of Mercy

I don't know what you were like as a little girl, having only seen a picture of you in your long, dark ringlets and drop-waist dress of the twenties. You already had those gently arched eyebrows that never needed shaping.

Whatever prompted you to become a nurse was to become your downfall. Perhaps your stubbornness, strong will, and thinking that you could do anything without anyone else's help were what did it; or perhaps it was to make up for your mother's death. She had died of complications from childbirth when you were still an infant. Someone later cruelly remarked, "Oh, you're the little girl that killed her mother," words which echoed in your ears forever.

Since your oldest sister had already married, the second oldest became the mother, of necessity. She lavished her love and caring on you until she was taken ill with a painful cancer, and you reversed roles and nursed her until her death.

You nursed cases diagnosed as "terminal" back to life more than once, and eased the going of many more. In doing so you gave up not only yourself, but your one, true love (a life you had saved when everyone else had given up on him) for the sake of church law.

Children turned you on. You could have had a dozen and would have loved every minute of washing grubby hands, splashing with them in the lake, and feeding them goodies. Once you confessed, "If I had it to do over again, I would have married the first man that asked me."

You took care of everyone else in the family beginning with the thirty-five year struggle with your brother's multiple sclerosis. There were others in the family, but you didn't need help, or so everyone thought. Being up in the night with him and doing the running of the household for another brother and frail sister, who was unable to help you, but somehow could ride horseback and run a social service agency, took its toll.

You probably needed help to stay awake in the night and help to sleep when you got the chance, and eventually alcohol became your greatest helper, anesthetist and support. At that time nobody realized that a person can't do round-the-clock nursing care without relief. But you did it; and when that stint ended, you cared for your remaining brother until his cancerous death, all the while following the directions of your sister and carrying out her elaborate menus. In between times you went at a moment's notice to swab a child's sore throat or to give a visiting relative her daily insulin shots.

When they were all gone but the frail sister, and nobody else needed you, the alcohol took over. You absently closed your head in the cupboard and burned dinner to a charred ruin that bonded to the pans.

I began to hate you for what you were doing to yourself.

Once as I pulled you, with a cut ear and sooty hands, out of the fireplace, the only thing that finally stopped your incessant activity was holding you close and saying, "I love you, Aunt Helen. I love you." I just then realized that you didn't do this to yourself, but life had done it to you. You had given everything you had to everyone else until there was nothing left of yourself.

When the syndrome had destroyed your body and your mind, all that was left were your beautiful arched eyebrows, your long, still-black hair, a vacantly pleasant smile, and pure love.

And, finally, you were gently taken down from the cross.

Vacancy

Alone,
I unlock the door
to the cottage of memory,
and you are there.
Through the picture window
the lake is a scene
from a travel brochure.
Indoors,
all is as you left it.

Nostalgia draws me to the organ
where I finger favorite songs;
and within the music
I hear the children's
happy banter on the waves,
imagine you perched
on the black sitting-rock
in the shallows, dandling
the baby on your knee.

Your laughter
accompanies the melody;
and as I play, the sun
dapples the dining table,
lighting the candelabra
for a phantom dinner party
only you could host,
and the notes become tears
which water memories
in the cherished chambers
of my heart's cottage.

Night Flight

You say, "Let's welcome
the New Year in the air!"
So I sit behind you, brother,
as your passenger
in mutual celebration.

The takeoff liberates us
from our mundane cares; we veer
from twinkling lights of town
toward youthful haunts:
woods and fields we both enjoy.

Above: a chalky, full moon.
Below: snow-covered landscape,
purple-gray, bathed in silver.
Our shadow glides across the land
like a manta ray on the ocean floor.

The plane seems to dematerialize.
As droning motor fades away,
I seem suspended in timeless,
boundless space, acutely aware
of my oneness with all creation.

Just Be Cuz

My cousin started ahead of me
by five days.
My cousin was sophisticated
at the age of nine
and had boobs, two beauties,
by the time we were thirteen.
While I was still trying
to figure out how
to skate an eight
without falling on my flat chest,
she was playing spin-the-bottle
and self-assuredly riding her own horse.

Her branch of the family tree was polished,
while we just seemed like folks.
One grampa had a farm to die for,
and the other had two homes,
one in Florida—on an island.
Mine were dead.
Their house had a third floor
with front and back staircases.
We had a crawl-hole
in the back of our basement.

Twenty years later
when I was a teacher,
she was a school principal.
Even now, after sixty-two years,
she has had two husbands,
while I am still on number one.

When we get to heaven,
I just know she'll be
in charge of arranging
delightful social events,
while I struggle to write
the invitations—in verse,
before going back to the stacks
in the heavenly library
to catalog seraphic records and
Dewey-decimalize the books!

On Beauty

Cinder block walls and
cobweb-cornered ceiling
surround me as I'm
stationary biking
in our basement.
I give myself
a self-coached pep talk:
"Focus on your goals!"
Then as I grimly stare
at the concrete floor,
before my tire
a mica-fired glint
of inspiration glows
star-like before me.
How much beauty there is
in unlikely places
obscured by webs and dust,
poverty and homely faces.

You called tonight.
Who could imagine such beauty
in a telephone?

Weeding

I bend and stoop, grasp and pull,
strain to wrench the deep tap root,
play tug-o-war with the stubborn clay loam,
finally unscrew the root
until the root hairs yield to their dizzying ordeal.
I ignore the sweat trickling down
and the small bugs harrying;
more will only take their place.

Looking down the rows I see our son
in a red muscle shirt and
brown canvas pants gathered at the waist
to fit his slim form.
He could be an Alsatian farmer—
his great-great-grandmother would know him
as one of hers were she here today
or we there then.

We stop to wonder at a draft horse shoe
that surfaced after years of tractor tilling.
Was it from Belle, the blind horse that
great-great-Uncle Val drove to turn the furrows,
sweating as he walked behind her,
gently guiding with the reins?
Or maybe it's a silent message
from great-uncle Cass, now passed away:
"Don't leave this land to anyone else.
Love it. Cherish it. Husband it."

(cont.)

Our son pulls them more easily than I,
shaking the tenacious dirt from pale roots
that hang down flopping
like the necks of freshly killed chickens.
He places them on the ground root up,
so they don't willfully re-grow
like we transplants from the old world.
We are stronger than they,
but the weeds outnumber us.
Which will give up first?

Levitation

Face, torso, knees and toes
form a chain of islands
in a tranquil, tropical sea
of soft, Lake Huron waters
as I float on my back,
hands behind my neck,
chest slowly rising and sinking
to the rhythm of my breathing.
Water presses up from below
as if to reject this land-creature
out of its element;
but I'm content to stay
so as not to chase away
a weightless, lime-green dragonfly
which has mistaken my knee
for a landing stone.
    Lacking my extra layer
of feminine fat,
my son, lazing on a tube,
wonders aloud, "How long
could you float like that?"
"Perhaps long enough
to fall asleep," I say,
"on a day like today
with no waves on the way…
long enough to marvel
at this perfect summer day
when time, like my atoll,
seems suspended
in limitless space
in this idyllic place
on the face
of this placid,
sun-blessed,
blue planet."

Ring Presentation

These rings we now wear
were begun as you waited
for the right time to appear.
Their luster weakly reflects
the glow of my wanting you,
    hoping for you,
      waiting for you.

May they be reminders
of the bond that we share
as sisters-daughters-mother.
And though these rings
may wear away some day,
our invisible love connection
will endure forever.

Departures

"Le retour fait oublier l'adieu." - French saying
   (Returning makes one forget goodbyes.)

Daughters, son,
I would keep you forever.
Indeed, I do hold you
in my heart, protect,
savor and treasure;
but the visit must end.
Now you wend your way
to homes away from me.

My consolation is seeing
invisible threads like
fairy tale crumb trails,
that will guide you back
again and again.
(as if you could forget
the way from wherever.)

Inside, though, there are pride,
satisfaction, and confidence
that you will flourish independently
when I am the departing one,
leaving unseen heart-lines.

Real Estate Magnate

Rich in properties I am.
As I survey my vast estate
I marvel at its accumulation:
It started small, when at an early age
an uncle gave me a plot of his time
and planted there some budding skills,
nurtured with his love of nature.
My father brought words home
from his newspaper office
to add to my fields of experience.
An aunt took cuttings from her passion
for trees, transplanting a rich portion
in my wood lot.
A swampy corner of my land is filled
with sunny marsh marigolds—
scattered by a mother who shared a love
of beautifying seemingly unproductive ground.
Oh, I cherish my holdings even more
because I know that it has all been given
in love to tend and pass on to others.

On Turning Sixty

This morning I am sixty.
Only yesterday had fifty begun to fit.

Today grampa's eyes peer from my mirror
to discover my father's frame
with mother's round head atop.
Her skin, with the tan she never wanted,
loosely covers bulging, blue veins,
and her hand grasps the brush
that smoothes my grandma's long hair.

The real me is in a curled photo:
on the beach at summer camp,
jackknifing off the three-meter board,
swimming through a carefree life,
skate-carving a figure eight,
energetically juggling a career,
a husband and three youngsters.

I turn from the mirror
to look for the children
that I love to take for walks,
to play with in the game room,
and nestle on the bed to read.

The house is empty.
It, too, belongs to someone else.

Friends

Friends Are Like That

Beanie babies:
soft, plush, lovable.
Select only those
that strike a chord
on heart strings
without compulsion
to amass a complete set.
Remove all labels and
appreciate their uniqueness.
Enjoy each one
for its individual spirit,
that feeling of well-being
and peace in its presence.
Gather them around
when in need of comfort.

Ready or Not

Delightful fright
quivers my skin
as I crouch under
the spirea's umbrella spines,
ready to flee if discovered.

My childhood friend,
eyes pressed to forearm
leaning against the maple,
intones the chant,

"Five, ten, fifteen, twenty…"
  ..ready for shoes?
  ..ready for school?
  ..ready for dating?
  ..ready for college?
  ..ready for exams?

"twenty-five, thirty, thirty-five, forty…"
  ..ready for a career?
  ..ready for marriage?
  ..ready for babies?
  ..ready for meetings?

"forty-five, fifty, fifty-five, sixty…"
  ..ready for leadership?
  ..ready for volunteerism?
  ..ready for grandchildren?

"sixty-five, seventy, seventy-five, eighty…"
  ..ready for retirement?
  ..ready for leisure?

(cont.)

"eighty-five, ninety, ninety-five, a hundred…"
  ..ready for eternity?

"Here I come, ready or not!"

Not!   Not yet.   Never ready.

Infiltration

These aliens walk among us
unobtrusively. They speak
as we do, affect our mannerisms,
even master our language.

One moved into our neighborhood
when I was ten...said she was
from Altoona, **PA**, which was
an omen unrealized until
years later, when I moved
to **P.A.** (Port Austin) Another
one was from **Pa**ducah, Kentucky.
Nothing is coincidence with "them".

Through casual association
she cleverly concealed
that she was here to teach me.
Over the years, patiently
by her example she taught me
to be non-judgmental and acceptant.
She modeled constancy,
friendship, openness,
solid ethical, moral conduct,
unspoken, unconditional love
worthy of emulation.

I didn't see the accidental clues
that might have betrayed
her true identity: she ran
with inhuman speed
and played an old piano,
never having had a lesson.

(cont.)

We grew up.
She waved goodbye and stayed behind,
never letting on that she would never
release her power over me;
while I, oblivious, went on for years
believing my good fortune
to be my own doing.

Then one day, in a book that explained
their covert operations in our world,
I saw the code name, "Donna Grace"—
the one who operates under
the Archangel Uriel.

Yes! They walk among us!
If you listen with the ears
of your spirit, you may hear
the barely perceptible rustle
of angel wings.

Tick In Time

This last time we met—
it seemed a lifetime of years
and four children—
we found a booth
at the back corner
behind our present lives.
Before our order came
we had regressed
those fifteen years.

Giggles at our childhood pranks
turned into explosive snorts
as bursts of memories
exploded into hilarity
over the time we skinny-dipped
and were stranded behind the big rock
submerged in water to foil the
mosquitoes and avoid being caught
that dusky evening of our adolescence.

As the music on the old juke box
changed from country to new age
we recalled the secrets
we had only told each other,
our hearts swelling at the realization
of the faithfulness of deep friendship
that time nor distance can diminish.

(cont.)

You saved your biggest secret for last—
the news of your life-threatening leukemia
flashed a vision of eternity
through a fissure in my heart
to reveal the brevity of our lives
as one tick in time.

Allow Me to Introduce...

Folks, may I keep this puppy?
    He needed to be found;
he's cold and lost and hungry.
    Don't take him to the pound.

            Mother, here's a friend of mine—
                I think she's really cool.
            She's an awesome tennis player
                and in the band at school.

Dad, this is my classmate, Bob;
    we're partners in chem lab.
We're going to the beach today—
    I think he's really fab!

            Girls, this is Mary Alice;
                her interests are like ours.
            She'd like to join our garden club—
                her specialty is flowers.

Students, this is Hennika,
    who has a tale to tell.
You'd never know she's foreign;
    she speaks our tongue so well.

            Honey, here are Mark and Jeanne—
                they're into horses too.
            Give them a tour around the farm
                and show them what you do.

(cont.)

There's someone special you should know
    that I've admired along the way;
he's bright and kind and talented.
    What's that? Yes, he is gay.

                                Look who I brought home today,
                                      I wanted you to meet—
                              She's jobless, black and homeless
                                  and living on the street.

Mystic Mentor

"Creusa cried for, through the tomb of Troy.."
                          Claire McAllister's "Aeneid", 1955

We coeds in white bucks and pastel anklets
    listened, mesmerized,
    as the doe-eyed face
    beneath the long tangle
    of tousled, sandy hair
    softly shared its ethereal verse.

Oh, if we could be this mystic maiden of the moors
    in heather skirt and flowing hair and voice.
Oh, if we could comprehend the words she spoke.
Surely, she had spent her youth in walnut-paneled libraries
    communing with Sir Walter Scott and Nesta Higginson.

What was Creusa up to – was it on the Via Roma?
I should have looked it up, but
    back in my bleak dorm room above the convent
    I sometimes sang lustily in a husky Mae West slur,
    "Give..Me..What..Croo-oo-sa Cried for..
        In..The..Stree-eets of Rome,"
    as I bumped and ground.

Drydock

Witty, sophisticated, experienced,
he was back in college from the service
with a real five o'clock shadow.
She was a high-school-to-college student
in pastel bobby socks that matched
her cashmere sweaters.

After she turned twenty-one
he took an interest,
picking her up after class
in his used convertible.
They docked at the "Yacht Club,"
but she never saw a ship,
just their pictures next to
fake portholes on the walls.
The only rope moored the bar
to an imaginary pier where
aqua glass vessels contained liquids
instead of displacing them.
They might have made waves
had they swizzled more vigorously.

To a small-town girl
this was sophistication—
weren't cocktail glasses essential
props in every movie with any class?
They were his prop;
booze was his leading lady;
he romanced alcohol,
danced with swizzle sticks,
flirted with voodoo vodka.
Olives enhanced his love
…for martinis.

People who cared about her
gently warned her, hinting
that he would eventually be
a deckhand on that intricate ship
in a bottle; but she couldn't hear
over the roar of the motor.

Finally, her ego wearied of being second mate
on a phantom ship on a becalmed ocean.
She longed for real salt spray upon her face,
the challenge of the open seas,
sunlight and starshine,
a chantey other than
"Yo-ho-ho and a Bottle of Rum,"
and being able to scan the horizon
with clear eyes and a light heart.

So one bright day
she shoved off.

Mirror Image

At a college get-acquainted mixer:
   "I've seen you somewhere before.
   Do you work at Alpine Drugs –
   out on the northwest side?"

At a parish bazaar:
   "Aren't you the clerk at Alpine Drugs?"

Before French 101:
   "You look just like the girl
   who waits on me at the drug store.
   She's really nice."

Who IS this person whom I resemble?
What do I look like to others?
Does my mirror tell me truth?

Curiosity draws me to the bus stop.
I transfer downtown and take
the northwest city bus.

Opening the door to Alpine Drugs,
I am greeted by a very pleasant voice.

   -   -   -   -   -

She is really, REALLY homely.

Desecration

We quietly climb
    the rusty-orange rock dome
    of our special mountain
    to celebrate in silence
    and awe the moment when
    the sun surprises
    over the distant peaks.

Three sister hags arrive
    gabbling, babbling,
    cackling about the time
    Daddy got drunk
    that Thanksgiving,
    and was it Aunt Phoebe
    who farted during grace
    before the Christmas dinner?

A bull elk bugles up the sun.
    The summons reverberates
    across the valley
    intoning the perfect mantra
    as we sit in tune yoga-style;

and the crones smash
    this quicksilver moment,
    shattering and scattering
    the fragile fragments,
    which skitter into the cracks
    of our last, precious morning
    on the mountain
    together.

My Friends Pretend

My friends pretend that
   they're not busy
   when I need to talk,
   that they were going anyway
   when I'm out
   for a three-mile walk,
They claim my not-quite-tasty muffins
   are just the most delicious,
   even when I make them
   overly nutritious.
They find my recent poetic efforts
   ever-so-inspiring,
   and my favorite jokes
   they've heard before
   are never, ever tiring.
They never protest when I insist
   I know just what they need,
   even though my directives
   they don't always heed.
They let me drag them as I run
   from gallery to mall;
   all this says they love me --
   wrinkles, warts and all.

Inconsistency

Someone asked for help the other day.
It wouldn't have taken me long,
    but my hands were full with helping myself.

Someone needed a ride last week,
but I was going a different route, and besides,
    I needed solitude to think.

Someone needed to talk through a problem,
but I was on my way to play,
    so I put their tears on a back burner.

Yet today I paused on my timed bike ride
to carry a turtle across a busy road to safety,
    magnanimously preventing its demise.

Strangely, though, in my den I spend my time freely,
studying lofty spiritual books in an effort
    to chart the philosophers' paths to Heaven.

Social Creatures

Just before sundown
geese honk a syncopated
chorus of various notes as they rise
from their afternoon rest on the lake.
They seem to consult each other
about the best flight path
to their favorite cornfield for dinner.
Once in formation, they chide
each other good-naturedly,
contentedly gabbling as they flap
their way under the clouds.

We women board our bus
for the return trip from
a pleasant theater experience.
The happy murmur of friendship
becomes a celebration of sisterhood.
Dark settles, and the murmur
drowns out the drone of the motor.
As melodic soprano and alto voices
of varying volume and tempos
intone thoughtful discussions,
exchange of ideas, future plans,
and memories of shared experiences,
the volume escalates, punctuated
by outbursts of laughter.

In the morning I gather eggs.
The hens in the chicken yard
cluck and chatter as they execute
their scratch-and-peck feeding dance,
contentedly secure in the sorority
of familiar fowl.

Evolution Runs Rampant

On her way to a bridal shower
for her daughter, and realizing
that all the others would be
young, twenty-something,
career-women-mothers,
she wondered what she could
offer conversationally
of common interest.

Will they talk babies, potty-training?
She couldn't remember which stages
occurred when, nullifying
her mother-mentor status.
On the topic of fashion and décor
her country/traditional/eclecticism
would impress like corn pone
amid these neo-modernists.
Regarding the entertainment scene,
she would be *Gone With the Wind*.
In gossip about friends, liaisons,
engagements, marriages, divorces,
she would certainly tune out.

But at the shower
introductions were soon followed by
discussions about the value of work,
educational methodology,
sociological theories,
the relationship between family trends
    and the breakdown in society,
the psychological needs of children,
dealing with interpersonal conflict,
pressing women's issues, and
current calculations supporting
    the big bang theory.

(cont.)

In a flash, she realized
the big bang is now.
It happened between her generation
    and her daughter's.

High Time At High Tea

When we women get together,
    it's more than merely tea;
it's caring and sharing
    and camaraderie.

It's not just the hats
    and the jewelry we wear;
it's more about friendship
    and letting down our hair.

Oh, the scones are great,
    and the sweets are good,
the tea is fragrant;
    but it's not just about food.

It's retrieving the leisure
    of our childhood past,
and revealing the secrets
    that make friendships last.

It's reconnecting
    with sisters and mother
in a warm celebration
    of our love for each other.

Garden in the Rain

Basking in the sunshine of celebration
we sip our scented tea,
    savor the flavors of friendship,
    share stories and ideas.
We pass around photo-memories
    of a grand European tour:
    beautiful buildings,
    impressive vistas,
    grandly groomed gardens
    of England, France, Switzerland, Italy.

Here at Eagle Bay, Michigan,
thunder rumbles,
and the artistry of rain and lightning
enrich the green of trees and grass.
Looking out the open door,
    I see the garden,
    vivid with clean whites,
    yellows and rich purples,
smell the freshness of the perfumed air.

Could the Luxembourg Gardens in Paris
be more beautiful
than these shastas and hostas
dancing to the soothing rhythm of the rain
on this pleasant summer day
right here at Eagle Bay?

Cat's Cradle

Friendship ties woven among
the "Straight Eight" circle of friends
pattern relationships like string
looped around eight upright fingers.

Secure, reliable lines link
Ann, Carla and Joan, forming
vigorous, shared bonds that foster
mutual support and steadiness.

Knotted and jumbled cords
from confidences violated
confuse and tangle connections
between Janine and Alyssa.

After many false assumptions,
jealousies and competitions,
frayed threads, taut and fragile,
put Joan and Glenda at risk.

Droopy, dust-covered strings
loosely moor Ellen and Susan,
while fine filaments forebode
disjunction for Glenda and Ann.

From time to time they slip
a finger here or there
as they re-loop and re-group,
creating new configurations
in this social cat's cradle.

Liberation

The world pressed against me.
Little by little I built a shell,
opaque, to hide myself
and protect my sensibilities.
A thin film at first,
it thickened and hardened,
muffled the world's clamor
and numbed my senses.

Through a tiny peephole
I saw you, harlequin,
dancing in delight
in spite of doomsayers,
mocking the masses
with your painted face,
bright, electric eyes
and ecstatic smile.

And our laughter
shattered the shell
and scattered the fragments
like a shower of confetti
around my feet,
leaving me open
to the warm sunlight
and lilac-scented breezes.

Amazin' Grace

Sometimes when I lie awake
my brain will do a little quake,
and I ponder, "For goodness sake!
What's so amazin' about Grace?"
It could be the beauty of her face,
artistic talent all over the place,
that deep-down goodness in her soul,
her maddening tendency to cajole,
her adherence to her goals,
or her aptitude for glee;
but the really amazing thing I see
is that Grace
        puts up
                with _me_!

Path of Least Resistance

The path of least resistance
has led me to this quagmire.
Left to myself
I flounder in the quicksand
of my selfish desires
and impetuous choices.

As I desperately grope the air,
the saving hand
of your inspiring example
is miraculously there.

Ricochet

Once there was a little girl
whose mother gave all her love
and all her care and attention
to everybody but her family.
The little girl always wondered
why her mother didn't have enough
love, care and attention left over
for her.

The little girl grew up,
married, and had children of her own.
All the love that her mother
had sent out to others returned
to the daughter through
her husband, her children
and the many friends who
admired and loved her.

And she lived happily ever after.

Goals

This girl I knew
was always going to church,
    was always going to be a nun.

My best friend said
    she would never make it;
but I knew she would because
she was always going to church,
    was always going to be a nun.

And she may well be ... but

the last I heard,
she had run away to Pennsylvania
... with an ex-con.

I guess it wouldn't do to be
    always going to marry an ex-con.

lemming revolution

i had a friend
who was the arbiter
of taste and style
and whom everyone
naturally followed

this went on
for years
a given

but little by little
she branched out
into life styles
choice of jobs
and child-rearing

i made the break

freedom was heady

last week she
was wearing her hair
just like mine

Enid

Enid of the kindly face,
filled with otherworldly grace,
touched the lives of countless students
and taught her colleagues gentle prudence.
When turmoil came upon the scene,
she maintained an air serene
as others wrung their hands and ranted.
Enid bloomed where she was planted.
Surely she pleased her creator—
we'd do well to emulate her.

Ayun

"Ayun" aged,
but her youthful outlook never wilted.
After her open-heart surgery
she just slowed down enough
to smell the flowers on her walks,
to take an active part in meetings,
to play bridge, to write poetry,
to encourage others along the way,
to share her whimsical insight
with many old and younger friends.

Like a perpetual grandmother clock
she taught the value of time
until that day at fifteen minutes to ninety
she put out her trash, returned to her home,
and her pendulum stopped.

Bob

It was years before I learned
that his real name was "George";
"Bob" seemed to fit him better.
He liked when a newcomer
said he looked like Marlon Brando.
All the people he knew
fit into two categories:
old friends and new friends—
and then there was a third group:
friends he hadn't met yet.

He had long enjoyed drawing,
especially old cars and old buildings
and later decided to add watercolor
to his list of interests, saying,
"If I make a mistake with an old car,
who will know that it's not
just a dent or a patch of rust?"
His sense of humor made him
comfortably welcome and
drew others into Finan's Store,
where they lingered at the fountain
feasting on the latest village goings-on.

He is missed in all the familiar village places.

Liz

Like a nightingale singing in the dark,
Liz lived through many dark nights
of disappointments, difficulties and
pitfalls that would disable and defy
the efforts of even the strongest;
yet her spirit sang in her poetry
and spilled out onto the canvas of her life.
Quietly and unobtrusively she painted
a depth of devotion to her family,
a love of God, and an appreciation
for the beauty of this world.

Like the nightingale,
her inner voice sings on
in her poetry and art
and in the hearts
of her family and friends.

The Harpist

Spider, Indian totem of creativity,
weaves her wondrous web
of transparent filaments
visible only in angular light,
when bedecked with glistening dew,
or shuddered by struggling prey.
Do her footsteps on the grid
emit inaudible vibrations?

Gentle harpist in flowing gown
sits at her celestial instrument,
mesmerizes with enchanting emanations,
and draws us into a captive trance.
Gazing at her movements
see the harpist's hands scurry
spider-like across the strings,
fingertips plucking, to weave
a wonderment of heavenly sounds
as she magically entraps us
in the mystique of music.

Truancy

to a purple-shaded
corner of my soul I go
to pluck each bead
from the inside-out
trident pansy pods

deep in milkweed
cushions curl
and spoon life's
minty pollen
from a peanut butter jar

under leafy arbor
whisper in
a cricket's ear
my secret
sung on raspy bow
to his own love
by degrees

on a toadstool table
in my mind's lab
I dissect words
rearrange their DNA
to express the feelings
only non-words say

some day
I may
invite you in

Grand Theft

My friend loaned me a book today,
and I devoured it right away—
digested it so eagerly
    that it became a part of me.

As I gave her back the book
I tried to hide my guilty look
so she wouldn't see within
    my secret literary sin!

Elementals

You, my friends,
are rain and sun,
wind and soil to me:

refreshing drops of rain
that cool my fever,
wash my wounds,
and pelt my mind with ideas
to stimulate my life;

healing solar rays
that warm my soul
when the unkind world
chills my spirit;

airy gusts of wind
that dry my tears,
whisper encouragement,
and swirl around me
with consoling caresses;

rich, nourishing soil
that sustains my life
and offers a solid foundation
for my heart's home.

Farewell

Whenever you leave,
    a part of you stays.
You're remembered
    for the style of your ways,
and the goodness of you
    on our heart string plays.

But you're no less whole
    when you leave part behind
because if you look,
    you're bound to find
a part of us goes with you, too.
    It's how we're designed.

Neighbors

(Deception)

My new car isn't really new,
but it's newer than my old one;
and it's a secret because
it's the same color and style
as the old one;
so nobody knows
I'm driving a new-to-me used car.
Outside, it's kind of stodgy—
a sedan like old folks drive.
It was previously owned
by a well-to-do lady who died,
then by her cool son,
who wouldn't be caught dead in it.
But interiorly speaking,
I'm smug, because inside
and under the hood, what the public
and the neighbors don't see are:
a turbo-boost, dyna-jet motor,
adjustable steering wheel, car phone,
electronic, automatic everything,
leather seats that remember physiques,
and a super-woofer stereo system!
Village life being what it is
and everyone wanting to know
everybody else's business,
if the neighbors realized,
they would just die!
(Let this be our little secret.)

Feral Roses

The farm house is abandoned now.
    Bare, grayed wood and broken windows
    lend a skeletal effect.
Mossy, worn shingles
    present a futile shield
    against the weather.
Thick weeds surround a tangled climber
    as if to protect this last vestige
    of life and beauty,
    the only hint of life and warmth.

Who were the tenants who planted this vine?

The more recent owner was a crabby fellow.
    "I could shoot that horse
    right out from under you,"
    he called matter-of-factly
    one day as I rode by on the public road
    that passed his posted, fenced farm.
    Any access trails into his swamp
    had been barred
    by strategically felled trees.

That was years ago, before the final abandonment.

        (cont.)

But the rose;
    somewhere long back
    there had been love and laughter
    amid the struggle and toil
    of clearing the land
    and building this farm.
There must have been children;
    this crabby fellow came from somewhere.
There had to be hope
    that built the now-decaying outbuildings.
There surely was love
    that planted the rose.

To Make A Shack A Home

The house next door
was built on four pine stumps.
A rough-textured crazy quilt
of tar paper, wood panel patches
and fake brick siding
holds the shack together.
Fortunately, it is almost hidden
behind untrimmed hedges
invaded by insinuating trees
and groping grapevines.

The property is a wart
on the face of a neat neighborhood
on a gracefully curving village street.
In the former garden
strong-willed ivy and brambles
have knitted a blanket cover
for wild and feral rabbits.
The only vehicle is a rusty wagon
parked beside the door, waiting
to haul the weekly groceries.

Yet every Christmas
the aging, old-country inhabitants
of this shack built on pine stumps
invite their neighbors in
to warm their hearts in the glow
of real candles lighting a real fir tree
in a corner of the one-room shack
filled with love.

Good Neighbor Policy

Shortly after they moved
into the house next door
built on pine stumps
he called as we were going to work,
"Hey, neighbor, why don't you
just go fishing like I do every day?"
"Can't. We have to work."

His battered old car
became a junker, and he
pretty much stayed home,
maintaining his connection
to the outer world
via high-powered C.B. radio
augmented by a rooftop wire thing
that resembled a huge raptor skeleton
pouncing on their sparrow shack.
He bragged that he could reach Charlevoix,
then extended his reach by mounting
an outside speaker, a powerful probe
invading homes, privacy, lives
with his garbled invectives,
cutting out our TV reception
always at the point
of Johnny Carson's punch lines.

He issued proclamations:
"At 1400 hours on August 8
I will force the closing
of all U.S. Air Force bases.
Prepare to evacuate the premises."
      and
"You people in the blue trailer
are on my property. As of today
you owe me six thousand nine hundred

and fifty dollars in back rent.
Pay up by Wednesday, or
I'll electrify your trailer."

When they didn't pay the "back rent",
he shuffled his huge, flabby body
across to their mobile home
and nailed the doors shut
with them in it.
The police convinced him thereafter
to stay on his own property.

For years he lived like a turtle,
only emerging on sunny, warm days
with a blue porcelain saucepan
like a helmet over his baseball cap
to ward off dangerous alpha rays,
fallout, and acid rain.

He never wore underwear,
(ask me how I know);
but now he must have read
about boxer shorts being "in"
when worn "out"
because when he comes out
on a sunny, summer day
aided by a tobacco-stained walker,
he wears a winter cap, ear flaps down,
a flannel shirt with a brown juice smear
down the front, a hunting vest,
black boots, and—boxer shorts
with a brown stripe up the back.

(cont.)

When he works his walker toward our yard,
I activate my good neighbor policy:
I say pleasantly,
"Hello. Nice day, isn't it?"

But I lock my doors.

The Web

Suspended like a spider
in the space between our bushes,
eyes penetrate my awareness.
Outdoors any hour of the day
her cobweb gaze clings
stickily to my clothing.

The inevitable "HI-I-I-i-i-i,"
as she shuffles across the lawn,
one foot turned askew,
spidery arms hanging
almost to her knees.
With one snaggletooth
in a mouthful of pink gums,
she is a crone who seems to wear
a pack beneath the back
of her sweater, collector
of dog hairs and varied lint.
Dog odors, fuel oil
and scent of sweat
vie with her greeting
for my attention.

(cont.)

"HI-I-I -i-i-i," she repeats.
"Where were you yesterday?
I thought I saw you leave
in the morning at 6:23.
Who was in the green car?
She left it in your driveway,
and you went somewhere together.
Would you save me the obituaries
from Wednesday's paper?
My sister's friend's neighbor died;
I met her once when we lived near Lum;
her boy was in school with our son."
Her questions are spidery filaments
winding around me,
restricting my life.

Extending a gnarled hand
she pleads, "Would you trim
the nails on my right hand?
I can only do the left."

"Would you contact the Red Cross
and find out where our son is now?
My Christmas card came back
from North Carolina.
That's where he was stationed
when he returned from overseas."

Empty, hungry eyes absorb me,
drawing me into her web-checked face
nestled in gray, straggly hair.

"I'm having trouble with Elmore.
Sometimes he can't get up,
and he thinks people are trying
to take our house away from us.
He wears that pot on his head
so acid rain won't damage his scalp,
and he messes, you know.
I had an extra orange,
so I brought you this one."

Through a screen door
behind the hedge
a heavy voice booms:
"Godammit, you bitch,
where's my friggin' lunch?
You've never BEEN worth a Goddam,
and you'll never BE worth a damn!
They oughtta take you out
and cut your friggin' HEAD off!"

She hunches her shoulders
and scurries back to the web.

By The Numbers

    23rd - this day in September
    55 - the degrees of air temperature
    62 - the degrees of Lake Huron water temperature
    18 - the wind speed in miles per hour
    1 - the number of freighters on the horizon
    56 - the number of geese overhead
          flying south in V formation
    7:28 - the time in the morning when my neighbor
          went down to the lake to bathe
    6 - the number of items of apparel
          that she wasn't wearing
    29 - the number of crew members on the freighter
          regretfully unaware of this beachside scenario
    7 - the number of times she dipped her head
          in the lake to rinse her hair
    72,000 - the number of goose bumps on my skin
          as I observed this phenomenon
    35 - the pounds of pressure exerted
          in wringing out her washcloth
    4 - the estimated number of reasons
          for this ritual
    4^3 or 65,536 – the level of my wonderment

137,560 - the totality of what makes life interesting!

Pilfered Plum

Caught red-handed
and red-faced
as reddish-purple juices
ooze toward my chin line
and stain fingers that still
clutch the contraband pit
of the juiciest plum ever.
    The owner of that tree
    so near the road
    stormed up in his pickup
    to inquire did we know
    whose tree this was?
Truth is, we hadn't speculated
on that—just figured
whoever it was wouldn't want
the ones on the ground anyway.
But possession of a pit
is no-tenths of any of the laws
the land-owner quoted.
In reply to his convincing rhetoric
we backed away,
mumbling apologies.
    May the serpent never slither near
    with a plum in his fangs,
    or I'm doomed.

No Stupid Questions

Shock of white hair
over red-splotched face,
shrubby white eyebrows
snuggled like sleeping kittens
over preoccupied eyes,
full hands that looked
as if they had mended
their share of fences.

I remember Robert Frost.

He was my first celebrity.
I had expected God;
but here he was,
not at the pearly gates
but at the farm gate
that I opened to receive him
into isolated Camp Hanoum,
my heaven in Vermont
the summer of 'fifty-five.

As the college-student counselor
with an English major, I was
given the honor of greeting
my greatly admired poet
along with a warning that
he didn't tolerate stupid questions.
Deafened by my heart beating
the words, "No Stupid Questions!"
on my ear drums, I welcomed him.

We walked the golden lane
past riding ring and archery range,
covering all that could be said
about New England weather;

then up the sun-dappled path
winding through the woods
as farm life was the topic
until this unsophisticated twenty
and a very ordinary eighty
in black, baggy pants arrived
at the open-air meeting hall
that looked out on Hemlock Mountain
across the cloud-dappled lake.

He recited simple poetry
to a host of eager campers
and wearily answered questions
from five- to fifteen-year-olds.
I wanted to sneak inside his mind,
plumb the profundities that lay
incubating there, sit at his feet
collecting cast-off metaphors
and leftover scraps of rhyme and meter,
seine his soul for secrets of syntax,
and adopt his yet-unborn imagery;
but "No Stupid Questions"
clanging in my brain
rendered me speechless.

Then he left on ordinary feet
wearing ordinary old-man shoes
leaving me strangely let down
with the realization that
real people exist behind
the facades of fame -- real people,
who get gravelly-voiced as they age,
scratch their noses when they itch,
and don't tolerate stupid questions.

Casing the Casino

Entering the casino,
he goes left to play;
she goes right to while away
the time reading by the fire;
another is parking the car.
I case the place:
the cashier's line is long—
do I want to spend my
allotted hour in line?
Passing up the line to find
a poker machine, I spy
a vacant stool 'way at the end.
That machine is o.o.o.
(out of order); its lights are out,
and I am o.o.l. (out of luck).
Looking closer
    this neophyte notices
    the only slots seem to be
    for the insertion of a card,
    which necessitates returning
    to the cashier's queue,
    which has now lengthened.

I decide to fold 'em
even before I hold 'em.
My eyes are sensitive to the smoke
of burning money, especially
when it's mine;
so I sit in the opulent lobby
and people-watch:
elderly on fixed incomes,
people in wheelchairs,
or aided by canes, crutches
    and oxygen tanks
hoping to be healed, or well-heeled,
gambling addicts looking for a hit,
down-and-outers seeking
to be "up-and-in-ers" or at least
find relief from their woes,
high-rollers-in-training
dumped in the smoke-free
kiddie game room while
parents bet their futures.

Fun, fun, nothing but fun!
Step right up and lose yer buns!
If it's so much fun,
why is no one smiling?
Grim faces tell the stories
of hopes dashed,
    of another week of work
to rebuild one's stock
of gambling money
and renewed hopes.

There's a man
who still has a penny
in his loafers—are there
no penny slots?
Here's a man in shorts and tee with
black business shoes and no socks
(can you hock your socks?)
figuring odds on his laptop.
It's a modern day game
of "Cowboys and Indians"—
but this time the Indians win,
and the cowboys lose their socks.

Mother Earth's Boy

Here's to you, Recycle Man!
You're up and out
before dawn stretches
her rosy fingers in the east.

You sort and re-commission
the used pleasures of our lives:
cans that provided savory delights,
papers now cold with stale insights,
bottles that warmed our social nights.
You rescue them from the garbage heap
and raise them to new heights
as offerings of our visible signs
of commitment to planetary stewardship.

Your work is more than a job—
it's a noble mission
to preserve the planet,
a pursuit of lofty worth.
Surely you are a favored son
of Mother Earth.

Cleaning Lady

A cleaning lady beknownst to all
is remarkably clever and equally tall:
she can wax the floors while washing the wall;
and had you inspected where she swept,
you would agree she is totally ept.

Jody
(at the poetry reading)

discovering sex
young man ejaculates poems—
penile penmanship

Disconnected

Today I tried to share
five different, compelling ideas
with my companions.
Each time I opened my mouth to speak,
three other people started talking.
I only tried once for each idea,
stubbornly refusing to beg
them to listen.

I suppose the world isn't any the worse
for being deprived of my innovative idea,
my gem of wisdom,
my unique insight.

But strangely,
bits of drivel,
foolish prattle,
humorous nonentities
captured the full attention
of the group.

My telephone has no mouthpiece.

Paranoid Painter

The color that I choose is blackish blue.

My rosy sunrise dries to shades of puce.

The brightest flowers lack luster,

and the muddy sunflowers droop.

A smiling face looks sadly grim,

and the hands extending love to me

reflect the ominous color of death.

Between the Cracks

In the arid gravel
along preoccupied sidewalks
among cast-off cigarette butts
and broken bits of life's chaff
which provide neither nourishment
    nor encouragement
nor reason for existence
out of sheer persistence
there survives, even thrives,
    great beauty.

Some call them wild carrots
    for their tap roots that auger
    deep in search of moisture;
but others, captivated by the intricacy
    of the delicate white, lacy flower,
    know this regal European beauty
    as Queen Anne's Lace.
The queen's blue sailor came along
    to flavor her coffee and simply serve:
    endive-leaf chicory hovers nearby
    with cerulean flowers whose heavenly hue
    belies the stem's toughness.
He nor the queen will ever be seen
    drooping. Bravely they try
    to hold their heads high;
    and should you attempt to remove them,
    their tenacious roots
        and rope-strong stems
        will prove you a fool.

Between cracks of slum playgrounds,
   beside shadowed doorways,
   amid deprived conditions,
   in spite of neglect
   and poor treatment by man,
   our beautiful children survive.

Dear Callie,

I love you.

Now before you say, "Weird old woman!"
it's not like you think.

I love you,
even when I drag you
from forbidden places;
push you, protesting,
to be all you can be,
I love you.

But you're doing this to yourself,
grinding yourself into the dirt.
And I love you.

A lot of people do.

Your teacher

       p.s. to Callie

    Now you're pregnant.
    I ache for your situation;
    but now is where you are…
    not what you did,
    but what you do
    and who you want to be…
            where you go from here.

If You Believe in Crickets, Rub Your Legs Together

Alone
in my campus basement apartment
without husband, children, or pets.
Alone – and feeling intimidated
by raucous men across the hall
behind the ever-open door marked
with mysterious, secret symbols,

I stock the food my family wouldn't eat,
make three day's worth of one-dish ratatouille,
and study until early morning.
As sleep sifts around me,
Bigfoot returns to the room above,
thumping across my ceiling for hours,
leaving me sleep-deprived –

and alone.

One evening a cricket chirps a bid
to sublet my lonely domain.
I must evict him (like the previous tenant's pet
excrement that lay dehydrated in the closet).
On hands and knees I prowl the premises
and find innocent beady eyes peering out
from makeshift hearth under the stove.

We strike a deal:
I will pay him in lettuce-leaf lucre;
henceforth he will be My Cricket.
He will tolerate my ruminant monologues,
sing me soothingly to sleep at night,
and leave my cotton clothing
alone.

Beauty Salon Visitors

dressed in silk leisure pants
for "at home" elegance
patent leather purse
gold-heeled pumps
hair style from college days
image counts

up drives yellow jeep
half hour late
nature girl jumps out
barefoot to reveal toe rings
ankle bracelets jingle
tight biker shorts
old grubby Wyland tee
weather-beaten face
thatch of unruly hair
calloused hands
aging former hippy

tall older woman
slim of shape
shorts and fanny pack
unaware of varicose veins
or doesn't care
earned them

real woman
overweight
baggy knit slacks
rag socks and Birkies
faint scent of garlic
knows who she is
what is there to say?

Beastly Beauty

The painted lady flaunts
   Botox-injected lips,
   Cleopatra eyes,
   padded buns,
   augmented breasts.
She throws her image
   back at her creator, pouting,
"You should have done a better job!"

Meanwhile,
   crow's jet feathers
      glisten with midnight sheen;
   'possum's pink nose
      complements fur of gray;
   the common dandelion
      is content with merely yellow;
   and clover attracts the bee
      with its own sweet perfume.

Hats Off to Women!

Hats off to women
    who kept tent fires burning
while praying their hunters
    were safely returning.

Babushkas off to women
    who toiled on the farm
as they cooked and sewed clothing
    to keep children warm.

Veils off to the women
    holding covered heads high,
giving others 'round the world
    the courage to try.

Caps off to nurses,
    selfless to the core;
and snoods off to riveters
    who served during war.

Now doff mortarboards
    to teachers, whose dedication
has made progress possible
    through improved education.

And bras off to those
    whose obnoxious confession
made us aware of
    our sexual repression.

And here's to the women
    whose bold declaration
won for the rest of us
    our proud emancipation.

Here's to all women
    who answer their call,
causing good things to happen.
    Hats off to you all!

Label-Maker
(I know who you are!)

That Herm is critical to a fault,
and Elaine is always spouting Gestalt;
as a wife, Trish is purely ornamental.
Dar and Trevor are so judgmental.
Count on Daphne for slipshod work;
and Perry, well, Perry is a jerk.

With Priss, the perfectionist,
    there's only HER way,
and Jocko is learning impaired -
    what's there to say?

Kit is the town's most prolific talker,
and Bruce has the mind-set of a stalker.
Muffie is clueless, or on the border;
Milt has attention deficit disorder.
Ben's hang-ups render him unable,
and Sonny is emotionally unstable.

As these caricatures come to the fore,
I don't see beyond them any more—
just label everyone on the fly.

My sole enigma is: Who am I?

Relationships

Love Knots in the Thread of Life

With the fragile, fraying thread of life,
one complication can provide the knife
that severs the tenuous filament.
The single strand turns flimsy and weak
lacking the faith and strength we seek
in solution to our predicament.

Kindness appears from everywhere
as neighbors rally to show they care
enough to support our fraying spirit;
and each kind deed ties another knot
which combines to provide the strength we sought
to re-knit the thread with hope inherent.

Burdens shared are burdens lightened…
darkness shared is darkness brightened…
and love shared is love heightened.

Gifts...

      wrapped in satiny ribbons
            festooned with balloons
                or curly-cue bows
      colorful strings attached
            some almost invisible
                spider filaments
                      designed to ensnare.

Benevolence

A rose knows no pretense.
It can only be a rose,
and that is enough.
It accepts its nature
and shares its true beauty
and sensuous scent
with any color of eye,
with any shape of nose.

While we—
we complicate it all,
sharing our smiles stingily
with those we deem worthy,
while those who most need them
go wanting.

Snake-in-the-Grass

Snake in the grass,
you crawl on your ass
with surprisingly minimal torque;

and you are among
those who smell with your tongue,
which resembles a tuning fork.

Strangely enough,
it's the very same stuff,
a stick-like fork, that will trap you.

And when you tire
of your present attire,
your skin decides to unwrap you.

On a medical pole
or down in a hole
is where your friends can find you.

You can shimmy up
for a claret cup,
(processed from apples, mind you)

or slither down
with nary a sound,
and an attitude *never-you-mind*,

but better beware
of that female fair
with a serpentine axe to grind!

Vulnerable

I am a naked snail,
a defenseless slug,
tentatively testing
each turn in my path
with sensitive tentacles.

Frowns. Put-downs!
Carping criticism.
Abrasive words!

Feelings bruised,
I retract my feelers
and withdraw,
wishing for
a hard shell
like real snails have.

Meanwhile
my salty tears
are dissolving
my entire being
into a frothy
nothingness.

Public Domain

Listen, prying reporter,
I do not buy your tabloids,
do not care to be fed
the intimate details
of lives of people
whom I neither know
nor wish to know.

Yet, in some there must exist
a feverish voyeurism,
because you flourish;
and now your blight spreads,
spewing its lurid trash
into my home
through the media funnel.
It clutters my life space,
chokes me with its glut.

But most unsettling
is the probable possibility
that irretrievable bits of **my** life
may lie nakedly scattered about
on someone else's junk pile.

| Between The Lines |

In my childhood as father guided the car
between the lines on the highway,
I would gaze out the window at the homes
lining the road like books on a shelf
waiting to be read.

I would read the rustic thoughts
of the girl in a pinafore
as she milked the goats
beside an old farm house.

After rounding up the dogies
I'd enjoy sourdough bread and beans
in a rugged ranch house
ringed by well-populated pastures.

In a log cabin by a wooded creek
I would sweep the dirt floor
as I tended a pot of stew
simmering in the fireplace.

Behind the iron gates of an estate
I would play with the fancy dolls
of a poor-little-rich-girl
who had no other friend but me.

In the parlor of a colonial mansion
I would read a Southern belle on a settee,
bloomers peeking out below hoop skirts
as she demurely embroidered a sampler.

I rode the private elevator
to a penthouse where, eyebrows arched,
I elegantly smoked a cigarette
through a gold, pencil-slim holder.

Ah, when I was a child
I savored each house like a well-read book;
but now I am older, and sordid news accounts
have rewritten my comfortable scenarios;
so I don't read houses any more
for fear of finding hunger, neglect,
abuse, incest, murder or robbery.

Now I stare at the sterile, empty spaces

between the white lines on the pavement.

Awareness

At birth no one told me
the pressure I'd feel,
and the pain of light in my eyes.

When I ran through my childhood
no one explained
growth pains as I grew to my size.

I learned for myself
the yearning for love,
uncertain of finding that other;

and no one foretold
what love would entail
as bride evolved into mother.

Through history and now
in shocked disbelief
I have witnessed man's cruelty—

life came with no warning
that others' pain
would also be felt in me.

Alchemy

Turning a compliment
    into a barb,
changing a kindness
    into suspicion,
the paranoid alchemist
transforms his base *mettle*
    into fool's gold.

Attitude

Reality is whatever I choose to think,
and my thoughts are my choice;
so if I choose to think that
everyone revels in my pain,
then it is truth for me.
Conversely, if I choose
to assume that people are kind,
that is my reality.
The difference lies within –
it shapes my happiness.

Life's Little Lessons

Life, a tough teacher,
raps us on the knuckles
and makes us do it over
until we get it right
to teach us a lesson
that helps us see the light.

Agnes, doer-for-others,
couldn't switch roles.
To accept another's kind deed
would put her in jeopardy
of losing the kingdom.
Now other saints
spoon puree in
and wipe feces off.
Rap!

Hilda, tower of power,
was weak in tolerance.
The only aide who stayed
was patient, wise and gentle—
and very black.
Hilda's crumbling turret
tumbled her down
among the masses.
Rap!

C. W. Morgan needed to run
everything and everyone.
No one had a choice
or disputed his decrees
until one fiat failed
and the alcohol syndrome
negotiated a corporal takeover
to become the new CEO.
Rap!

Phoebe faked fainting spells
to avoid mundane chores,
but organized orders
for the drones to carry out.
Now her body stumbles,
refusing to follow orders
as others wipe her drool,
and she wishes she could help.
Rap!

Adipose Rex, gourmandized
and indulged himself
in dessert before, with,
and after dinner. Now
he wears a gouty crown
bedecked with renal stones;
and layers of gold chins
rest upon his chest.
Rap!

Here she comes
with the ruler,
nearing inch by inch;
get it right the first time,
or prepare to flinch!

Not Hap Rap

I'm so mad at the human race!
Why don't y'all get outta my face?
Ya dis me every hour of the day—
Just let me do things "my way."
Every time I turn around,
You're grindin' my ego inta the ground;
So why don't you take a flyin' leap
And throw yourself on a garbage heap?
I'm so mad at the human race—
ALL of you…get outta my face!

Ode to a Paper Clip

You smug little darling
rounded-off rectangular wonder
organizer extraordinaire
justice of the piece of paper
valued by
    perfectionists
    nit-pickers
    secretaries
    harried librarians and
that pain-in-the-ass math teacher
with too much time on his hands
who sits on my desk to chat
when I've the most work to do and
smirking, mindlessly
clips you and your cohorts
into a chain six feet long
so that when I need you a.s.a.p.
I must locate where he hid the chain
and wrench you free
all the while trying to restrain
the assortment of curses
piling up on my tongue lest
they erupt loudly here in a library
full of students who will
turn the tables on me and
fingers to pursed lips
hiss their collective
    "SH-H-H-H-H-h-h-h-h!"

Poet vs. Computer

My hero, my friend,
together our capabilities are limitless;
we can explore the world,
develop in ways never dreamed.

Our relationship showed promise
of productivity and growth,
but we're from two different worlds:
I'm too firmly planted
in the soil of earth,
and you're in cyberspace.
Can a marriage of earth and ether
blend successfully?

Right now our love is turning
to resentment on my part—
frustration born of misunderstanding.
Your responses are often tangential,
eliciting another configuration
of problems.

We need therapy, you and I,
or we're headed for divorce.

Song of the Sportsmen's Auxiliary

In beautiful autumn, the fall of the year,
our men go a'hunting the partridge and deer;
and then in the winter, (yo ho!) in the winter
on poker and bowling attention will center.
Then comes the spring – ah, glorious spring:
time for smelt-dip and baseball;
    they give golf a fling.
As summer arrives, that warm tourist season,
fishing robs them of all reason.
Thanks be out of any more seasons we're duped,
or our husbands would be completely pooped!

My Love Flees With the Northern Breeze

Picture the goose season if you can:
our home life creeps forward – sans man;
the storm doors are off and the screens still on;
the retriever is growing tired and wan.
The drains are plugged and the furnace won't stoke;
the clothes line fell down, and a shutter broke.

When my spouse is loose,
both the goose and her gander
   get my dander!

The Compleat Angler's Incompleat Wife

The breeze from the lake blows soft and mild
to stir the heart of my man-child
'til the spark in his eye is kindled wild.
No longer can my love immure him;
voodoo nor drug will ever cure him
as long as a fish is there to lure him.
It's a bitter drink to quaff:
I've lost my better half!

Subterfuge

Spouse leaves the house.
Door closes.
QUICK!

Pen a poem…

Wax your upper lip…

Play the piano…

Nibble a bon-bon…

But leave the vacuum cleaner
prominently plugged
within ready reach
when garage door rising
signals his return!

Distraction

You sit in the back row
    in a chair that remains unoccupied,
for you are somewhere else in your mind.
Beautiful teenager, capable of more
    than my efforts draw out.

I reach for your mind, but you respond
    with partial or missed assignments.
I try to show you a world
    that awaits your talents,
    your best efforts;
    but you are listless.

I think, *If only kids would get*
    enough sleep, a good breakfast,
as I surreptitiously search for bruises,
    outward signs of abuse.

Today I learn of your father's
    pawing and probing;
and through my tears, I wonder
    how you manage to leave
    your haven here at school,
    how you force your feet to carry you
    to that place that other kids call "home."

Your bruises are hidden inside—
    your "homework" written
in indelible black-and-blue ink.

Weight of the World

Can I sleep
   knowing that wars are being fought
by boys my grandson's age?

Oh, may I sleep
   and dream that altruistic intelligence
leads the countries
toward peaceful co-existence?

And may I sleep,
   while seismographs and meteorologists
are measuring the next impending disaster?

How can I sleep
   when images of poverty, hunger,
cruelty, abuse, neglect and unjust imprisonment
replace those of pristine sheep?

Will sleep finally come
   with hope for the rising of a friendly sun
to brighten the spirits of a new tomorrow?

I may sleep
   when I let Justice hold the balance scales
for God to assay and weigh.

Equality When?

Where is the hope, where the dream
   that women will reach equality?

Third world woman works with her man,
   and while he rests, she fetches and totes,
   prepares and cooks for all the rest,
   bears the children and falls asleep
   only to rise and do it all over again.
   The uncertain reward is survival…
                              sometimes.
   A chattel, less than an animal,
   beatings are her birthright.
   No guardian angel to the rescue,
          nowhere better to go;
   locked into time and place and attitude.

Civilized, emancipated, advantaged woman,
   with appliances that free her to work a second job,
   a sophisticated version of the third world woman,
   working for less pay and token benefits
          legislated by condescending males,
   acknowledged by a church that accepts her work
          but does not allow full membership;
   protected from violence by law, but not in fact.

Different times, disparate places,
   but still – the attitude.

Games

Little boys play
with guns and swords,
shooting, slashing,
    swashbuckling;
and the victims rise
to laugh and play again.

Big boys call them
    war "games."

The games become reality.
They shoot and slash
and wield their
swashbuckling power;
but now the victims
    rise no more.

Each side becomes
    the loser.

Telempathy

look behind their eyes and see the hate
understand the anguish of their fate
heart-shell cracks from bearing its own weight

hear the jibes a continent away
of warring youth that never learned to play
life after year after month after week after day

ache the stomach pains like bloody knives
that carve the babies from unwilling wives
and cheat the children of their unlived lives

tie the heart string in a callous knot
desensitize to vicious polyglot
invectives curses slurs and verbal shot

to feel is fear to hear is pain
to see is searing acid rain
to really love your neighbor
seems utter angst in vain

"Do Unto Others…"

An explosion a continent away
resounds in the recesses of my brain.
It is the blast of bombs
that leave families homeless
        and children bereft.

Muffled footsteps echo in my ears
as countless walking corpses
trek from their homeland
seeking survival
        and a better life.

Verbal taunts and clatter of rocks
jar my sensibilities
as children perpetuate
vicious outbursts of hatred
        instilled by their parents.

Enraged, my soul screams out
the pain of thousands of women
mutilated for their gender,
and the sorrow of those
        sold silently into slavery.

The Golden Rule's final line
has been aborted and buried
with the remains of unborn children:

        "…As You Would Have Them Do Unto You."

Feral Dogs

Mistreated pets, unchecked,
discarded by their owners,
left to fend for themselves.
They are hungry and poor—
hungry for love and acceptance
and poor in spirit.
No longer respected,
they no longer respect.
It's dog-eat-dog as they snarl,
squabble, gnash, slash and tear
at each other over occasional scraps
of putrid meat discarded cunningly
by those who bait them on
until their venom festers within
and spews out on those nearby.

Humans, greedy for money and power,
pit one against another;
and the snarling, bruising hatred
consumes us…until…
      we go out of control,
      and the mob rules.

The Pimple

Deep down inside my being,
   from the heart, the core
   of my sensibilities,
   began an uneasiness.

The veiled hypocrisy of politics
   became transparent as
   the leaders supported the claim
   that the Emperor was
        wearing clothes.

His statements were naked,
   but the people saw clothing,
   heard strength; and his words
   were transformed by many minds
   into meanings that fit
   their dreams,
   dreams of an empire filled
   with might and righteousness.

In the meantime, my un-ease
   became a dis-ease
   as frustration festered
   like a tiny pimple
   on my chest.

People rallied and protested
   to keep a dead woman alive,
   seemingly unconcerned for
   those living souls who are
   imprisoned unjustly and
   entire nations of people
   who have lost loved ones
   to an unjust "mistake"
   by power that parades in the gown

of liberation and salvation
from suggested threats
of destruction.

Oh, we have brought them freedom—
freedom to die in a democracy
imposed by outsiders.

And my pimple grows to boil proportions
as I struggle to suppress hatred
for those who cause man-made disasters,
when we should be spending our efforts
in feeding the poor and helping those
who suffer from economic
and natural disasters.

What good are my high-minded thoughts
about loving God
and seeing the beauty in nature
when our country is happily barreling
downhill in a hand-car driven
by rash conductors?

I am one mute voice crying out
to a deafened crowd—
one heart struggling to understand,
forgive, and maintain serenity—
and the boil erupts from my heart
through my own chest cavity.

Ashes of Hatred

Years of love
    and children growing,
years of work
    and warm home-building,
years of service
    and sacrifice
to reach our goals
    and a life that's nice—
all up in smoke
    with one cruel stroke
by those who know us not,
    yet hate us.

Prisoner of Empathy

I close my eyes, but still I see
the bodies strewn and maimed,
    bloodied and killed by intolerance,
intolerance unleashed by fear of other,
unwillingness to accept other ways of thinking
by other brains created by the same God
    called by different names,
other ways of thinking that threaten the comfort
    of narrow belief secured
    behind doors of insecurity.

The bodies are fathers, mothers, babies,
    daughters and sons, brothers and sisters,
    neighbors, whose pain has ceased,
intensifying the pain in those who cherish
these dead—pain that unleashes more hatred.

And I cannot shut them out.
Through locked lids still I see them,
and shoulder their plight as my own.

My eyes are closed,
    but when will peaceful sleep come?
Rosy dawn arrives to open the door
    of hope for a better day;
but soon the cold light of today's reality
shines into the painful cracks of awareness
    of others' ongoing plight;
and in my helpless love I pray
    and pray, and in my heart
embrace those others who are so like me,
    but merely believe another way.

Galoshes

Leaving the soup kitchen,
I discover that the boy
who parked the Buick
left with the keys;
so I must walk
the anonymous trek
from Lower Manrow
to Upper Avenue.

But why am I wearing
huge galoshes
clogged with muck and mire
below my cashmere coat
on this stylish street?

Discreetly I discard them
only to discover beneath the first
another, cleaner pair.
The mud and mire are gone,
but I am still wearing galoshes.

Remote Control – Klik!
or, The Pen is Mightier Than the Sword,
But My Klikker is Quicker

I have dreams,
aspirations for world reform;
starting small with here and now,
my remote control will rule.

Telephone conversations that ramble on and…KLIK!
Toddler temper tantrums ranting irrationa…KLIK!
Epithets spewing from unfamiliar youths on…KLIK!
Junk mail offering endless lists of unparalleled…KLIK!
Charitable causes rending hearts with hopeles…KLIK!
Telephone calls soliciting who-knows-what incess..
KLIK!
Bickering small-town politicians trying to prove…
KLIK!
Violence and lewd entertai…KLIK!
Forecasts of impending ecological disast…KLIK!
Reports of racial hatred, ethnic cleans…KLIK!

Hey! Where did everybody go?

The Furies On Spring Break

The ancient furies scream loose
from some long-locked
Pandora's Box, howling
through the open corridor
under the domed plexiglass roof.

Lying-in-bed-questions
from the top floor bedroom:
Will the roof fly off,
or will it collapse on us?
When it goes,
will we be sucked out of bed,
or buried under a shroud
of rubble?

Now they pry on the dome
breaking part free, slamming it
against the loft wall;
they wrench off the orange awnings
and slide them screeching across
the abandoned parking lot.
They knock insistently,
rattling our bedroom door.

In spite of closed windows,
single hairs hanging over my eyes
are moving. I hold my breath;
they wave at me derisively,
taunting, threatening.
The impressive light globe
outside our door
offers itself as a bhoodan,
crashing onto the stairwell
several flights down.

Power is low, but turning the volume up,
we hear, "...the worst storm of the century...
...entire eastern third of the nation...
...inches of snow in Atlanta..."

Palm trees bend their backs
to the buffeting blast,
their fronds, parted like hair,
reveal pale scalps
of their stem-heads.

Now sirens scream back at the Furies.
Will they scream for us next?
We have filled pots and pans
with fresh emergency water.
I take a shower to escape the din,
but the persistent imps taunt me
through the ventilator.

We distract the younger guests
by playing Othello, turning the disks
from black to white, then back to black
like the wavering score
between the storm and us.

By the second day they are tiring,
only hurling light objects, like epithets,
in our direction. We walk around debris
remarking at the incongruity of icicles
hanging from the tropical palmettos.
Filing like geese to the nearby theater
for diversion, we watch Bill Murray
relive Groundhog Day.
What if this were our day to relive
until we got it right? As we emerge,
light snowflakes are skittering
like confused cockroaches in light.

Clutching our clothing to us,
we wend our way to the fitful beach
where stiff bodies of whelks, starfish
and sand dollars lie like victims of our war.

Finally we arrive at terms of a truce:
they will retreat to Pandora's Box,
and we'll clean up their mess.

Focus-Pocus

Late in summer twilight at the beach
mysterious lights appeared above the lake;
three there were that hovered, moved, then stalled.
Excitedly we speculated source,
built plausible suggestions as to cause;
but scientific explanation failed,
and we concluded: other-worldly laws.

Two aged fishermen were on the shore,
who looked not up from tackle, bait and lines,
but mumbled 'tween themselves in muffled tones,
apparently oblivious to the fuss.
Did they ignore because they could not cope,
or were they visitors who studied us?

You call to me in many subtle ways –
expressions, covert gestures, silent pleas.
My total focus on the job at hand
and other interests that absorb my mind
make useless ears and eyes that do not see…
or is it fear of losing self to thee?

Eau de Toilette By Any Other Name Would Still Be Toilet Water

Now comes a product
to appeal to the lover
of the natural –
perfume by the name
of Fresh Water.
Of course, it's *eau
de toilette*
in a cool, blue bottle
shaped like a rain drop
with a bubble bottom
by Henryon.

Now we who love
to stand in the shower
imagining ourselves
under a refreshing waterfall
in a primeval forest,
who dream of a plunge
into a cool, deep pool
below a rocky precipice,
who revel at the beach's edge
as waves slosh sensually
caressing our skin...

now we can have it all
in a 3.4 ounce bottle
for only $75.00.

Affluence Spoken Here

The gilded serpent
    slithers over the bridge into Paradise
        lured by the luxury of the manicured median
            past impressive façades of over-scaled mansions
        no longer noticed by satiated eyes

Nature has been golf-clubbed to death
    and her bounty sacrificed on altars
        incensed with the smoke of burning money

Coiling smugly, he basks in the golden glow

You Are Here →X←

Forget about yesterday:
   what she said,
   what he did,
   what they thought,
   what we scorned,
   what you planned.
That can ruin your today,
and today is where you are, here.
Here and now—the only realities
that you can hope to influence,
that lie within your grasp.

The past is dead
and cannot be resurrected.
If you chose to live there,
you could not change a word,
   a deed, an outcome.
You cannot go back and apologize
   for assumptions made,
   errors in judgment,
   thoughtless deeds.
Gone is gone, my dear.
   You can learn from the past,
   but you cannot relive it.
Remember, but do not regress;
appreciate the past and learn,
that we may make today
the best that it can be.
It's all you have for sure.

Future Perfect

Remember as a child
how you daydreamed and planned
   the perfect future--
how it seemed that it would never arrive?

When finally the shifting sands of the future
fell within your grasp,
   they sifted quickly between your fingers
   to become a sandy path
   marked only by vague footprints
   running through time.

In imagination the future is perfect,
   marred only by the reluctant awareness
   of the imperfections in today's reality.

In My Perfect World . . .

flies won't bite before a storm
all people will realize that Yahweh,
    Allah and God are the same
carbohydrates and fats will make me healthy
clothes will always fit loosely
I'll understand what crows caw about
    and what geese mean when they gabble
our leaders will work for the common good
politicians will be statesmen
poets will be paid handsomely for their work
no one will be hungry
advertising and campaign promises will come true
drugs will only be used to heal
patience and kindness will rule the road
toads will be recognized as the princes they are
peeling onions will be the only cause to cry
intestinal gas will be like pleasant perfume and
people will all be a lovely shade of golden tan.

Minor Aggravations

Why can't a poem strike
when I have nothing else to do?
It's irksome, like that one
rebellious hair that tickles
your face just when you're
about to solve a pithy problem,
or a lone mosquito in from Mississippi,
but now in the still of your death-black bedroom,
whining in his southern drawl,
"Whah daon't yew evah give ME as much bloood
as yew give that studly ho-erse-flah from Ahgentina?"

Oh, no, this poem was ready NOW
when I was not.

It's enough to make me run away to Omaha
with that handsome, itinerant driveway paver,
or maybe to Quanicassee with the somewhat homely,
but very persuasive roofer, whose deal
I struggle to refuse.

Or how about discovering a corn flake
shaped like Pennsylvania just after
I've brought it to my lips all milk-soppy?
It could've brought two hundred on E-bay.

Or those "easy-open" can lids that require pliers,
hammer and screwdriver to pop the top
(both yours and the can's)?

So I'm sitting here on the edge of the tub
writing this less-than-inspiring poem
because it knocked on the door of my brain
just as I was getting out of the shower
after cursing the stopped-up drain.

Peace

Peace is a golden mosaic
of fractured bits of unrealized dreams
    reconciled by time
and of an awareness that
    our wants are not our needs,
and that chance can often effect
    better resolution than planned goals.

It is composed of
    shattered relationships
    painstakingly pieced together
    by mature understanding,
forgiveness, and openness—
    of shards of memories
    from a happy and pure childhood
    and the love of family and friends.

Song of Life

Harmony is not attained
by one lonely note.
    It is the deep voice blended
    with the high and delicate
    in combinations of
    complementary tones
    that mellow the melody
    and enhance the song of life
    with its misery and its ecstasy.
Keys both black and white
play infinitely changing patterns
that imitate the ebb and flow
of the human experience.
    Harmony is enhanced
    by intermittent silence
    nestled in the spaces
    between the keys
    where peace resonates.

Dream of Peace

Beautiful people
different, yet alike
making friends among nations
sharing one planet…in peace.

   In any family
   the combination of genes
   produces a variety
   of features and talents,
   each one wonderful to behold.
   In the world family
   that shares this earth
   we stand in awe
   of the beautiful variety
   that each individual brings
   to the blend of nations—
   each one different,
   yet able to love and appreciate
   those who share and nurture
   this precious planet.

Love

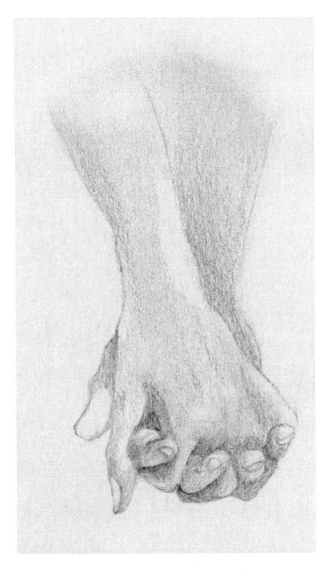

Overture to Love – First Movement
(at the weekly poetry reading)

His interest was piqued as she read
of wrestling her own private demon;
and then, unabashed, he spewed poems of love
with glances like cupid's arrows that zinged to their mark
igniting that spark seen by all those awake
who weren't turning inward admiring
their own reflections in cups of cappuccino.
A watcher's dark frown couldn't dampen the spark,
so the tinder caught fire causing admiration to flare;
and the smoke signal was visible and noted
across the miles by alert indigenous peoples,
who marked the moment on ceremonial moon sticks.
At that same moment dogs howled, not at the full moon,
which was doing its best to attract the attention of the tides,
but at the high-pitched frequency of taut heart strings
vibrating at rates detectable only by canine ears.

Now this obscure observer must wait in suspense
for the next week's installment of the burgeoning romance.
She must hide her intense interest in the study
of such covert body language while secretly yearning
for pyrotechnics spectacular and amorous vernacular.
Alas, she must put dreams on hold for the denouement to unfold,
knowing she's incapable of holding her breath 'til next week!

Quantum Learning

I learn.
The more I learn,
the more I realize
there is so much more to learn
than I can absorb in one lifetime.

Confusion marries chaos
and carries her over the threshold to my brain,
where they revel in untold delight,
    posing conundrums and playing
        at oxymoronic diversions.

The more I learn,
the more possible solutions suggest themselves;
and that duo in my brain locks the deadbolt
    on my mind's door.

Must I know?
Must I remember the Pythagorean Theorem,
grasp the Theory of Relativity,
be able to calculate trajectories,
    untie the Gordian Knot,
    crack the DaVinci Code,
and be able to quote Chapter and Verse?

Or might it be sufficient to merely appreciate
    the beauty of this world,
    to contemplate the wonder that is God,
    and enjoy love as it warms the soul?

Suddenly Truth

Suddenly and infrequently
an eternal, universal truth emerges
like a mushroom that appears
when you quit searching
and stop to rest--
there amid the camouflage
of last year's leaves
and storm-scattered twigs,
now settled, but reminiscent,
it sits, as if awaiting discovery--
or like a 3-dimensional picture
that eventually reveals
the sequestered scene or symbol
when you let your eyes go unfocused
and think of something else.
Meanwhile, contrary to my pleading,
time progresses. Yet
in the fleeting moments of life
that blur the vision to detail,
even in the changes—
the changing, yet changeless seasons,
the rhythms of the waves,
in the constant repetition of refrains
in life's varied melodies,
truth-- that beautiful, sad-eyed child
you didn't know was yours,
who appears in a dream,
and you become painfully aware
that you've never hugged him
or told him that you love him--
truth, like the mushroom, sits
waiting for that grand **eureka**
moment of discovery.

Who Would Dream...

..that the early rays of dawn could smell like dianthus,
..that stars could dance on the sea at midday,
..that the melody surrounding me could set the tempo of my heartbeat,
..that salty sea air could taste so sweet,
..that the postal service could deliver hugs in an envelope,
..that a sunset could paint visions in the Eastern sky,
..that a telephone could transmit serenades sweetly in my ear,
..or that the faded color of life's painting could suddenly brighten?

    I would...
        they could...
            they do... now that I've met you.

Convergence

      Handsome stranger.... through a window....

fleeting image on the street....

          a glimpse across a crowded life....

wondering if we'll ever meet.

*

Emerging friend... arranging meetings...

    delving deep into the mind...

        engaged in endless conversation...

           so intrigued by what we find.

*

Cherished husband .. now embedded ..
bonded by a common goal ..
sharing life and lively interests ..
integral to heart and soul.

Rendezvous

You will know you are near—
when the raucous ruckus of day
becomes the song of a meadowlark
landing on mandolin strings—
when the weight of the butterfly
delighting your shoulder
lifts the pressure
from the soles of your feet.

I will know I am there—when
the golden aura of contentment
disperses my shadowy cares
and the hair on my neck relaxes.

                      I will know you are there—
                      by the giddy goodness
                      that shivers my spine,
                      and the salty taste of fog
                      on my tongue.

I don't yet know where—
but I plan to meet you
…there.

Luna Love

What is there about the moon
that lovers rhapsodize and yearn?
The sun warms, but the moon
coolly reflects blue light.
Is it that the moon
seems unattainable,
like unrequited love,
its face bearing
that taunting, eternal grin?

But you-- you are sitting here
beside me; and the warmth of you
penetrates my jacket's insulation
to embrace my heart
as it eclipses my soul.

Dubious Certainty

Should best friends marry?
                                        And what about passion?
Compatible, yes, with much in common,
                    yet diverse in temperament and personality.
His reticence   balances   her outspokenness.
His calmness   tempers   her volatility.
His reclusiveness   is enriched by   her interests.
His precision   is enlivened by   her spontaneity.
                    But
        his master plan for the ideal wife
        did not include this intruder in his life
                            with her pendulous breasts,
                                firm, flat buttocks,
                            and long legs that place her lips
at his forehead,
            (In storybooks the ideal wife is engineered
        to stand on tiptoe to kiss her handsome swain.)
                            with her forthright honesty,
                            her adherence to personhood,
                                her lack of artifice.
            (Whatever happened to feminine wiles,
                the playing of coy games,
        a dash of subterfuge to keep the prey off-guard?)

                In the meantime she waits
        for him to discover what she already knows—
            that they are ideally suited to each other…
                                                her yin
to his yang.
His doubts   are not dispelled by   her certainty.
She is too tall for me
that's not the fashion.

Should best friends marry?   And what about passion?

Love's Litmus

If love is a feeling
>of well-being when together,
>of happiness in each other's company;

If love is having
>the loved one in mind
>even when apart;

If love is blind
>to the blemish, yet able to see
>the inner mark of beauty;

If love is respectful
>of other's ideas, body,
>goals and needs;

If love is thinking
>first of the beloved's needs
>before one's own;

If love means leaving
>space between
>so as not to smother the flame;

If love is doing
>what you can to make the loved one's life
>easier, better, happier, more fulfilled;

If love means wanting
>the best for that person
>even if it's not in your best interest;

If love means encouraging
>each other to develop
>and enjoy individual interests;

If love means knowing
>that you are a better person
>because of the relationship;

If love means appreciating
>the differences
>and celebrating the similarities;

If love means hoping
>for a long and longer life together;

If love means praying
>that you'll never have to say goodbye;

>Then I truly ___do / ___do not love you;

>and you truly ___do / ___do not love me.

Autumn (Spring) Weddings

Mature (young) love

    is a wonderful (frivolous) thing to see:

It's celebrated with (passionate glances and not)

    much serenity.

As two hearts (bodies) meet in synchronized

    (sexual) unity—

souls and minds (a new being) bond (dances)

    in (jazz-beat harmony) perpetuity.

Essence of Love

shared time, shared sorrows

joy in each other's good fortune

the essence of love

Spirit of Song

One clear voice,
like a clarion call at sunrise,
can awaken the mind.
Two voices joined together
vibrate the heart strings.
A blend of many voices in chorus
adds sweet, salt and spice
to the recipe of life, to delight the ears,
lift spirits, and join souls
in magical moments of music.
From our diversity we create
a colorful orchestra of voices --
linked in mind, in heart and spirit.
Awaken to the music
that announces the sunrise
of your spirit!

Scent of Love

Love is the sweet scent
   of God's breath on the world—
   headier than hyacinth
   boldly declaring its ardor,
   gentler than arbutus
   hidden 'neath last fall's leaves,
   too shy to speak.
Oh, envelop me
   in the blissful perfume of love!
   Let it cling to all I encounter
      on my way.

-- -- --

Calefaction

you brushed by
leaving lint
insulation for my soul

Wakeup Call

My eyes are closed in sleep,
yet the morning sun
seeps through heavy lids
to bombard the retina
with its bright message
of day's arrival.

So a loving smile
does penetrate my heart
with gently welling warmth,
which swells and overflows
to soothe and refresh
a worried world.

An Attempt to Define Love

Love is the realization
that our differences
fill each other's voids.
It is the comforting warmth
of your body next to mine.

Apple Antics

twisting the stem
working down the alphabet
with each twist
to devine the name
of your true love

mine was usually E
and I didn't know any
Edgars or Edwards
I did know a Eugene
but he was shy
and anyway
that was more like a U

it never occurred to us
that Steves Toms Uris
Verns Willards Yves
or Zacharys would be
unlikely true loves
under this system
although William
would have a chance
if you called him Bill

I married Edwin
it was meant to be

Adduction

You
have strength and solidity
to deal with whatever comes.
You do what you have to,
find quiet enjoyment
in daily tasks.
You're a pheasant fly-up,
a sky-line of wild geese,
changing seasons,
the birth of a foal,
a straight fence,
the neat pattern
of a properly mowed lawn,
a song with a story
that makes sense.

I
want to fly, to swim,
to feel the wind and water
in my hair and on my skin,
caressing, exciting.
I want a hundred
violins and flutes
to vibrate in my ears,
and clouds and trees
and flowers
to tantalize my eyes.
I want to play
with coins and clay
and velvet
and never stop.

Symbol of Love

The heart, a symbol of love,
pumps life-saving blood.
On tee shirts we see:
"I (heart) my bike."
"I (heart) chocolate."

While we might greatly enjoy
cycling or chocolate,
real love is demonstrated,
not by drawing a heart,
but through our hands—

hands that help build
a home for the homeless;
hands that work to provide
food for the hungry
and care for our families;
hands that soothe
another who is suffering;
encouraging hands that
applaud another's efforts;
hands that fold in prayer
for those in misery;
hands that comfort
a child's "boo-boo"
or nighttime fears.

Helping hands, encouraging hands,
healing hands, praying hands,
loving hands demonstrate
real love that's in our hearts,
not just on our tee shirts.

Actions Speak Louder

My words are as so much ink
   spattered across paper.
Separate from action
   and divorced from reality,
they become empty symbols
   of ineffectual ideas,
   weak expressions,
   unrealized aspirations
   and latent ardor
as they drag themselves
   across the page
   in meaningless patterns.

You publish no flowery passages,
   but your actions write clearly
as they fill pages of my life's book,
   expressing fidelity and constancy.
Your concern and care for me
   underline the simple,
   straightforward font.
Small, everyday kindnesses
   and thoughtful acts
   illuminate the script,
   embellish my days
   and serve to illustrate
        the depth of your love.

Cardiosophy

You… are the beat of my heart

   steady and true,

      that grounds and sustains me.

You… nourish my spirit

   and strengthen my soul.

Wherever I go

   I go not without you

      to calm and direct me.

You… pump my life blood,

   set before me a goal.

You… are the pulse of my being,

   the heartbeat of love.

Descant

Outside our bedroom window
in the dark of a rainy
spring midnight
a lone bird warbled
its varied love song
as if it knew what
we were doing
with our windows open.
It trilled on for an hour
in the middle of that night,
singing descant
to my heart's melody.

Haiku

Hearing the night bird

warble its varied love songs

I know happiness

Earth and Water

We are water and earth,
   my loved one and me.
I am the water
   that flows to the sea;
he the land mass
   to stabilize me.
Oh, what bliss
   it is to be
contained in his love,
   yet still flowing free!

Elation

Oh, world,
hold me in this day forever—
to celebrate the sunshine in my heart,
the multi-colored visual pleasures
    of nature
and the delight in companionship
    with my beloved!

Portrait In Ice

On virgin ice
I sketch your face
with the blade of my skates.

I start with a spiral
up the nape of your neck;
now glide around the fullness
of your silvering hairline;
changing edges,
etch the wavy furrow
across your brow,
and define your eyes
with a horizontal figure eight.

Slowly, fondly,
I sculpt your smile,
then careen around the ear.

Oh, if this flat, cold ice
could show the depth,
the humor,
the warmth that is you,
it would melt away.

Resonance

Your silent deeds of kindness

sing your love to me

in lyrics that join

with the music of the angels

to reverberate

in the chambers

of my heart.

Anniversary Song

I'm trying hard to know myself,
    but find it tough to do;
for when I look inside myself,
    I see so much of you.

Through all our years together
    I've learned a thing or two;
and one that I've discovered:
    a lot of me is you.

The love you speak, the care you give
    are reasons for this life I live.

You are often late,
    and I am sometimes crude;
and we have our differences
    in politics and food;

but one thing I've discovered,
    and I didn't need a shove:
we share the same in values,
    true friendship and our love.

The love you speak, the care you give
    are reasons for this life I live.

Although we often are apart,
    we're together in love true;
I wouldn't be the me I am
    if I hadn't married you.

Accompaniment

At the movies
oboes serenade with sadness,
drums echo fear pounding in my heart,
a lilting tune releases happiness,
and violins swell with love's discovery.

Out for a power walk
or pedaling my bike,
the tempo of my feet begins a beat
that causes me to snatch a melody
to match that movement.

Beat of feet,
hum of tires on pavement,
sound of leaves in trees
played randomly by breeze—
all create accompaniment
for the scenario of life.

But, sensing your displeasure
with my actions that don't measure
up to your ideals, the music fades;
and there is only deadening
silence.

Torment of Tantalus

Your smile sends messages of love;
    your eyes express it, too—
it surrounds you like an aura
    in the thoughtful things you do.

You're my faithful, loving husband,
    my friend of greatest worth—
so would SAYING the words, "I love you"
    halt rotation of the earth??

Q and A

Q's:

Who left the porch door open?

What are these papers doing here on the floor?

Whose junk is cluttering the desk?

Where did you put my remote control after you used it?

Why is the milk sitting out on the counter?

How long before you dust the furniture?

When are you going to get organized?

A: I'm living down to your expectations.

Legal Tender

You've been irked
with me before,
and it hurt;
but today I need a hug,
not criticism.
And when I try to tell you
about porcupine quills
that don't just jab
and slide off,
but work their way in
and fester,
in your frustration
you retort bluntly,
"If you don't like it,
why don't you move out?"

So in the criticism game
it's you 20, me 1;
and I lose
everything.

- - - -

I leave you a note,
my heart dripping
blood mixed with tears,
pack favorite old clothes
that accept me as I am,
throw some friendly books
into a rucksack.
I'll visit my sister
four hours away;
just say I missed her,
while I sort through
my old coin collection
of wounded feelings.

- - - -

At the halfway gas station
the attendant makes change
with a two-dollar bill.
There we are on my palm,
you and I, two ones
impossible to separate
without destroying the value.

I turn the car homeward.
Will the garage be locked?

- - - -

The house is empty.
My note is gone.
I busy myself blindly
shuffling papers at my desk.

A quiet footfall,
your presence beside me;
I get the hug
I needed all along.

In my pocket
the two-dollar bill
lies rumpled,
but still intact.

Considering Poetry

Poetry is the pounding hoof beat
of that horse the heart rides
through hollow caverns of fear,

the angry trumpet call
of the soul appealing
to the universe for justice.

It is the hymn of praise
sung by a happy spirit
bathed in pure sunlight,

the mellow vibration
of compatible heart strings
echoing the strum of love.

Magnetism

The glow of orange Sedona cliffs
attracts us to the vortices.
From the junipines a raven's chortle
carries through the clear air
signaling dawn in the mountains.

Aroused by the spectacle
of buttes and canyons,
we cuddle on plump cushions
pulled out on the porch.
In the distance, an elk
urgently bellows to his mate.

Red rock pinnacles
pique our passion;
and as you come to me,
that voyeur sun peers
over the purple rock ridge
as if drawn toward the heat
of our loving.

Orchestration

Your hip replacement mended,
my back pain abated,
our bed that seemed too small
has re-expanded.
As I lie gently next to you,
like reacquainting lovers
your goodnight embrace
strikes a chord that becomes
the prelude.

Gingerly, sedately,
we respond to melodic memories
of a former unfettered age;
and imagination becomes
the grandparent of two-part invention.
Subtlety and innuendo
compose the music of mature love
that orchestrates enjoyment
and unites the musicians
in soul-vibrating harmony.

Metamorphosis

Come to me, my love;
cast off your cares
    with your garments
and let love envelop us
in a shimmering, silken cocoon
to shut out the world
    with its impositions.
Succumb to the dizzying
    drumbeat of our hearts
and the heady perfume
    of our breath.

And when we've loved,
    lived, and laughed,
delighting in each other's touch,
we'll emerge, transformed,
on diaphanous pastel wings
to soar breathlessly
to higher levels of vision
and understanding.

Transcendence II

You have touched my soul
at the center of my existence.
My body fades away, insensate.
I am pure being, suspended
outside the universe.

Wired

Outdoors a cicada emits its
sizzling, piercing, high-wire song.
Half hidden by the pine tree,
the transformer on the corner
stealthily filters electricity
into our home, bringing
light, power for cooking,
warmth, sounds, and visions
that electrify my senses.
News of turmoil, crimes and dissent
infiltrate my life through silent sockets
as shoulders hunch to ward off tension.

Even sequestered in the silent
darkness of my bedroom
I am enmeshed in a maze of wires
that wait to surge their response
to the commands of the next day.

Then my beloved takes my hand
and leads me along the wooded path
toward the pond's calm waters,
where water bugs skate silently,
and frogs snooze with noses to the sun.
We stroll through pastures
where mares contentedly graze
as foals play foolishly at tag
with tantalizing butterflies.

Gradually the warmth of the hand
that cups my own diffuses my tension.
Serenity and solidity ground me;
and I return to the de-electrified me.

Take the Song

Take the song I'm not singing
   and give it your voice;
take this heart that is wringing
   and help it rejoice;
for the eyes that don't see
   and the heart without love
need light and warmth
   and a lift from above.

      Everybody needs some help from time to time
      to bring out a song and give it rhyme…
         and reason…
            when it's out of season.

Take the song I'm not singing
   and make it your own;
our song wasn't meant
   to be sung all alone—
for love is a seed
   that waits to be sown;
and the heart that's unfeeling
   needs to be shown.

      Everybody needs some help from time to time
      to bring out a song and give it rhyme…
         and reason…
            when it's out of season.

(cont.)

When life turns to gibberish
   and nothing makes sense,
there's a star to follow
   and a song for defense;
so keep music flowing
   though hollow the heart—
let this song reconnect us
   when we're apart.

      Everybody needs some help from time to time
      to bring out a song and give it rhyme…
          and reason…
                when it's out of season.

We Who Laugh, Last

Save the last laugh for me;
for now we'll giggle with glee
though red skies are warning
as we greet the bright morning.

In our milk we'll snort bubbles
when life hands us troubles;
'cause it's proven that humor
can dispel each dire rumor.

As life becomes serious
and events tend to weary us,
I'll bite dents in my knuckles
to stifle banned chuckles.

With belly laughs and guffaws
as life's gees and haws
yank us around at our work,
never a punch line we'll shirk.

Save the last laugh for us
as we weather each fuss
and glitch that knocks other folks flat
when they timidly step up to bat.

For it's high jinks and joviality
mixed with conviviality
that guide through the worst
to break a dread curse.

(cont.)

The last laugh – remember
as we near November,
and others lose the thrill
due to life's winter chill;

and though we're looking a sight,
we'll face Father Time's fright;
and we'll roar with delight
on our way to that final good-night!

Dance Trilogy

A One…

Dance with me!
Let the rhythm of our hearts
      provide the beat.
Now it plays a tango,
      pulsating sensually:
Dip me ardently, whirl me dizzily;
hold me intensely, twirl me busily!
And when it's time for be-bop,
      fun me, swing me,
      bounce and jive!
Ain't it great we're so alive?

And a Two…

In the dance of life and love
I go your way; you go mine.
So sway me back and lead me on;
I'll follow you wherever
the music in our hearts directs.
And if your feet stomp a polka beat,
I'll *hoop-i-shoop* with the best of them!

And a Three…

When the music winds down,
and that last, slow dance is played,
we'll shuffle around the dimming dance floor
with each other for support,
remembering the medley
of our life dance together.

Care To Dance?

Ah, those college years,
when we hokey-pokeyed around a beach fire
and Conga-lined our way through the cafeteria
to the "dah-dee-dah-dee-dah-dah, dah-dah-dah" chant.

At Arthur Murray's we followed step-maps
to enrich our repertoire while enjoying the scent of
Gene Kelly Wannabe's breath mints.
Inhibitions dissolved under the influence
of the sensual undertones of the Tango.
Choreography blended with geography classes
as my dizzying brain did the Samba in Brazil,
Fandango'd through Spain with a rose in my teeth,
and flapped the Charleston in the New Old South.

Infused with confidence, I enrolled in ballet,
mastered basic positions, even *pliés*;
but the *pas de chat* did me in.
After the wall mirror dashed dreams
of my tour with the NYC Ballet, I focused on
water ballet and figure skating.
I continued to wear the slippers
around the dorm, walking
with toes turned out.

A few years later I married a man who
neither ice skated, swam, nor danced.
On special occasions he could be wheedled
onto the dance floor
after a shot of liquid confidence.
We'd do a hesitant oberik, a jerky polka,
or an up-close, dreamy, slow dance that
didn't exist on Arthur Murray's floor charts.

Age and hip replacements turned polkas to a dirge.
After he died, my husband appeared in a dream to say
he wished he had danced with me more.

My dancing shoes are now dusty and stiff,
but my heart pirouettes wildly when he comes
floating suavely through my flights of fancy.

Top 10 Reasons for Staying Married 50 Years

10. You heard that arguing keeps your brain sharp.

9. You won't have to buy your wife a kaleidoscope; she can just watch you channel surf.

8. So you don't wake up to any surprises in the morning.

7. You can't teach a new dog old tricks, so stay with the old dog.

6. You successfully survived seven 7-year itches, so why scratch your marriage now?

5. You have someone else to blame for the messy bathroom/closets/basement/garage.

4. You're both too stubborn to let go.

3. Because it takes that long sometimes to decide if you really love each other.

2. You heard that if you do it with the same person 5,000 times, you will have an out-of-body experience.

1. Every time you remember what it was you were going to do, you forget your lawyer's phone number!

The Rose

The rose is over-bloomed
and faded cream, no longer yellow.
Look closer, you can see
its gentle imperfections:
an insect scar, a crippled petal,
failed symbols of a fruitful season.

Though life scars our lives
and changes touch us all,
love endures, remains unbroken,
a never-ending flower
beyond the reach
of time and place.

True Love

Love is about feelings and actions
   that are weakly expressed by words.

Love is about doing for other.

Love is staying power; it remains
   when everything else has changed.

When the loved one no longer remembers,
   love is still there in the lost memories
   of times gone by.

Sometimes
   love is just sitting with
   and letting be.

Loss

Undertow

The undercurrents of age are
   drawing me down
   more insistently each day.

In my panic I struggle more frantically—
The wilder I flail,
   the deeper I sink.

If only I had the courage to relax
   and go with the current,
I might float to the surface.

Birthday Buzzards

On my sixty-fifth birthday
six buzzards circled overhead
spoiling an otherwise glorious day.

      * * * * * *

Atop a fence post
reminding me of life's end
birthday buzzard waits.

Can merely being helpless be a prayer?

When you don't know how to get from here to there;
and love hurts so much
that it'd be easier not to care;
can merely being helpless <u>be</u> a prayer?

Ephemerality

Heavy with weariness
in the very room where I began
you leaned over the dresser
to seek relief from
the burdensome weight
of this new life
that would eventually
overshadow your small frame…

invoking gravity
to hasten the exodus,
anticipating the mighty rush
to release this budding life.

Finally, sweat
welling to a mighty flood,
you poured out your strength
as my being struggled,
gasping for its freedom.

* * *

Now as I look
upon your cold and empty
shell which held my chrysalis,
the chill of missing you
envelops me.

Apprehension

Waiting to register
at the desk…

waiting to take
the dreaded test…

waiting for
the lab to call…

waiting for
the other shoe
to fall…

We Carry On

Sometimes the prognosis
hits us with the stunning clarity
of sunshine on an icicle
that falls, pierces the brain
and wedges into the heart,
numbing the pain of knowledge.

Faces frozen in apparent
control and comprehension,
    we carry on and do
    what must be done.

As the heat of the heart's anguish
melts away the ice,
    it dampens the pillow,
    washes away the tension
    in torrents of tears,
    and bathes the soul in solace
as we carry on;
and through the fissure formed,
a tiny mote of light finds its way
to that deep place within
    where hope is born.

That tiny mote glows brighter,
and hope grows stronger
fed by the love that spawned it,
    and we carry on.

Don't Go

O bobolink, o cricket,
o miniscule arbutus,
if you were to disappear,
who would provide
your whimsical beauty,
your cheerful music
on a summer night,
your sweet, sensuous scent
to delight and inspire?

And you,
who would be my companion
to whimsy me when I am alone,
to hum a pleasant melody
and send me fragrant thoughts
when I need a gentle touch
and warmth of a loving smile?

Abraham Would Understand

"YOU CAN'T DO THIS!"
My clenched fist thrusts heavenward;
yet Isaac-like she lies on the sacrificial altar,
   the blade swooping,
                    testing.
No angel interrupts my terror.

"CALL IT OFF!"
My brain screams wordlessly
as deaf hands direct the ghoulish task,
   proceeding methodically
        through the well-rehearsed drama.
No voice offstage halts the hideous ceremony.

"Please, let me keep her."
My hands petition prayerfully
   as motionless she lies,
        oblivious of her role.

"But if life be worse than dying?"
My inner heart inquires, tear ducts trembling,
   as the mocking, murderous melodrama drones on,
        intensifying the supreme suspense.

"Thy will be done."
My nerve ends mumble numbly,
   exhausted from the grief,
        ignoring self-relief;

        (cont.)

my soul slumps wordlessly,
   quivering helplessly.

At last the answer—
  soft,
        whispering:

            "Amen."

"Streamline"

He rode into our village and married
the winsome widow Bea, who owned the bar,
which they renamed "B-Line"
in honor of their merger.
Because he hailed from "The City"
we were suspiciously wary of him;
after all, he was a "sheeny-man"
who bought and sold to his advantage.

Over the years, the sheeny-man's
charm proved deeper. His love for people,
his zest for life, were no sham;
the ever-present twinkle in his eyes
reflected genuine love
emanating from his soul
as he faithfully cared for her
until her death. His step-children
and their children were in turn
devoted to him and to his care
as his body – not his spirit—
grew weaker; though the eye-twinkles,
like sparks from a glowing campfire,
continued to kindle a like response
in those who knew him, until
he was raised to a higher plane
to shine among the stars.

Lessons From Angus Patrick Kennedy

Police advice: When on the street,
    don't walk the beat with too-swift feet;
pace yourself so they can see
    that imposing presence, which may be
        an influence for good.

Take time to let new friends acquaint
    with the life story that you paint
with Irish humor and dry wit,
    embellishing it as you tell it
        around the neighborhood.

Tread gently with your family,
    adding buds and branches to the tree;
proudly keeping track of progress,
    encouraging them in the process
        as they branch out on their own.

Support your sisters in their song;
    help your fellow man along.
Be there in their times of woe
    as up their own twelve steps they go,
        sympathetic to each groan.

Now enter into heavenly joy,
    as they welcome St. Pat's tallest boy,
who at the end has passed the test
    and finds himself among the best
        to walk an other-worldly beat
        with golden wings upon his feet.

Untimely Death

He was called away too early,
too young he was; and we
felt cheated by his passing,
for we had longed to see
all that he'd accomplish
for himself and society.

Now his plans and projects
lie dead and unfulfilled;
and our hopes and aspirations
for the future that we willed
lie with him cold and lifeless
as if they too were killed.

But our time is not God's time.
Though our hopes for him seem dead,
his present time is timeless; and now
in that place where he's been led
he knows that our dreams were weak
compared to the bliss that lies ahead.

To Theressa

In the flimsy light of pre-dawn
the stillness awakens me.

No bird calls,
no whisper of a wave upon the beach,
no rustling leaf,
no night creature shuffles,
no drone of traffic from the distant highway.

The earth's pulse is muffled
as it holds its breath
    awaiting your passage.
Your suffering and degeneration
lurk in the spaces of the silence.

Praying my uneasiness to sleep
is ineffectual in masking the deathlike hush.
The memories of you intrude themselves
as they rerun a silent movie of your life,
with its richness, kindness, devotion,
    understanding, talent—
and a certain serenity that said
you knew where you were going all along.

Necro-Feedback

Tomorrow I'm going to tell you
that you have to fight this thing
push yourself harder
don't take it lying down
give it all you've got, man!
(positive mental imaging
and a determined attitude)
Muster all your grit
    and conquer it!

But tomorrow
before I could say it
    you died.

Mr. Dodge

Once I was paid to work under a man
    for whom I would have worked without pay.
He was many things to me:
    administrator,
        leader,
            educator,
                humanitarian,
                    sage,
                        father-figure,
                            respected friend.

He didn't change under pressure from earthly powers,
    each of which had a different idea
    of who and what he should be.

He was tolerant,
    patient,
        kind,
            firm,
                loving,
                    gentle-humored.

He saw the good in people and treated each one as important,
    and they just knew he cared about them.

I used to dream that someday I would
    walk across hot coals for him,
        so he would know that he was all these things to me;
    but I never told him.

I wrote this poem and read it at his funeral,
    and we…almost…didn't cry.

Inhumation

Our steps slow to the tempo
of the dirge within our hearts
as we follow you this last time
into church.

Numb, we listen
as the well-meaning minister
strings platitudes
(like a child's awkward,
colorless, macaroni necklace)
that break and fall to the ground
without expressing the warmth,
the loving joy and kindness,
the welcoming hospitality
that was you.

Nutmeg-scented incense
envelops your casket
like a final, collective hug
before levitating with your soul.

Bereft, we weep
but for ourselves,
for you are no longer with us;
yet you are always with us,
will always be
in our memories
and our hearts,
which were touched by your smile
and changed by your life.

One-Man Dog

You suffered the pain
   as long as you could
   before your body gave itself up
   in spite of your moral strength.

Now I am a one-man dog lying
   at the foot of your grave,
   slowly starving as I wait for
   the stick to be tossed one more time.

Burn the good sheets;
   I'll use the shabby, worn ones
   that know so many nights of loving
   and dreaming a future together.

Donate the clothing to Goodwill;
   I'll keep an old sweatshirt to hug me
   on lonely days (every one)
   and your scruffy barn shoes by our bed.

Hide the trophies in a closet;
   they're painful reminders of
   exhilarating accomplishments
   that can never be relived.

Smash the special china
   on your gravestone,
   for what can ever be special again
   without you?

Grounded Phoenix

With one wing missing,
the other wing of a wooden yard-bird
wildly spins as I walk by.
"Foolish bird," I say, "You cannot hope
to fly with one wing!"
The words ricochet,
hitting me full-force on the rebound:
You cannot hope to fly with one wing!

Without you, I am a crippled bird
left with memories of our soaring together;
yet here I am in the attempt,
spinning clumsily in erratic circles,
buffeted by random winds
that only fan the ashes of my efforts
and do not lift me off the ground.

While I struggle to fly as before,
"You cannot fly with one wing"
reverberates louder than the sound
of my frantic flapping as I try
to rise out of the ashes of grief.

Fulfillment

When I was young I yearned
for something—I knew not what—
a something to fill
    an indescribable emptiness,
    an indefinable loss.
Perhaps it was a lover?
No, more than that—
    a bridegroom called "fulfillment."

You provided for my temporal fulfillment,
    satisfied my worldly longings,
    gave me children, purpose,
    freedom to explore the world,
    to develop in my own way.

Now you are gone from my sight,
and I look to The One Who Is Love
    to satisfy my longing
    and to reunite me with you
in that place of eternal fulfillment.

Loneliness

Loneliness and grief are raptors
that voraciously eviscerate,
yet leave the prey, invisibly wounded
to walk among others
unnoticed in its plight.

Only fellow victims recognize
the results of the vicious assault,
hear the hollow echo from within,
reach out to support the faltering step,
and try to fill the emptiness.

Sunset Song

You are the song my heart sings

      when it's filled to overflowing –

I am one abandoned by a sunset

      after its final stage of glowing.

Irony

As another wave of self-pity
washes over me in the darkroom of grief,
I try to develop the negative
in order to view the positive.
The photo appears in stark black and white—
it is a couple, and the face of one is missing.

Birth pains come in advance of joy;
but the price we pay for the bliss
of having loved and been loved deeply
is put on the extended payment plan.

Mourning Reigns

Renoir said black
is the queen of colors.
Suffering the king's death
is a cruel way
to earn the crown.

Giving Up

As a child I practiced "giving up":
    candy during Lent, pennies for the poor,
    the first half of basketball games
    so I could go to Mother of Perpetual Help devotions.
I even gave up a good boy friend
    because we were of different religions.
I'd give up wanting a cashmere sweater
    just to prove I could talk myself out of anything.
I offered up my physical pain
    for the joy of a baby's birth.
My practice so steeled me that,
    when our daughter was desperately ill,
    I could give her over to God with total trust
    even in my heart-wrenching distress.
Now I'm forced to give up you,
    and it's the hardest sacrifice I've ever made.

Pick a Card, Any Card

The game is Life, and you are dealt
   five cards – all diamonds:
   Daughter, Student,
      Career, Wife, Mother.

As the game progresses
   you draw many hearts.
You're sure to win, until…
   your partner is clubbed
   with the Pain card,
      and you follow suit
   with your Anguish card.

He draws the Death of spades
   and there is only one card
   remaining for you to play—
   the Loneliness of hearts.

Widowhood

Another black flower opens
in my garden of friendships;
its somber, dewy petals contrast
with brightly-hued surroundings.
It seems the sole dark spot
in the confetti-colored collection.

The black blossoms, once so rare,
are now proliferating;
yet each one stands out,
solitary in its anguish,
drooping visibly as if deprived
of water and nourishment.

Each new ebony bud drains color
from other once-bright flowers which,
diminished, pale in empathy and,
defying the sun, lean to support
these cherished blooms.

My Heart, My Love, My Life

Forty-nine years and five months ago
you caught my eye.
Soon after, you captured my heart
and sustained its beat,
and now you have been my life
for over forty-eight years.

You have completed me,
    filled in my blanks,
    supported me, been my anchor
    and my faithful, faith-filled counterpart—
    the yang that grounded my yin—
sometimes exasperating, but always you were you.
You knew who you were without having to prove.
You tolerated my ways,
    cherished me in unspoken deeds.

If you were a tree, you would be my oak,
rooted deep in the earth while reaching wide
to embrace and shelter your family.

No hands are as beautiful as yours—
strong for work and to protect,
yet gentle in caresses.

You are the only you there is—
    the only you for me.
You are my gander, mated for life.

Star-struck

When first we met in daylight,
starry-eyed, we explored new worlds.
Your brightness guided me on;
you were my sometimes faltering beacon
shining through the holes
in the aging mantle of my darkest nights.

Now, like a fleeting flash of comet
you have passed through my life,
and I am left to scan the cold night sky
beyond Alpha Centauri and Cepheus,
past the Andromeda Nebula,
seeking the light of your star
for warmth and consolation.

Floodgates

After your death
the lead-heaviness of my heart
crushed you from memory,
frigidly evicting you from thought.

Life filled in the vacant spaces
your image had occupied.
Children's messy hands
stirred the present,
muddying the waters of the past,
and overvalued mundane tasks
commandeered my focus.

Now, three years later,
on this steel-gray winter day
your old hunting hound,
lost for several seasons,
wanders listlessly home,
emaciated.
Warily entering the yard
he circles tentatively
as if unsure of my welcome.

He limps within reach;
and as I hug his bony frame,
unable to release my grasp,
those years of hoarded tears
wash clear the foggy window
of remembrance.

Disappearing Act

This evening the swollen, red-rimmed
eye of an orange sun slowly closed
in front of a sky draped in gray—
quietly, without a colorful display or fanfare.

Just so, my dear, you were
my scheduled, dependable sun
that lit my way and warmed my heart
on chilly days with simplicity of style
and true, contented to be just you.
Unhurriedly you lived your life
then left too soon, mutely masking strife
to spare your wife the tribulation.
One would think such silent passage
                           would leave no gloom,
but as I search from room to room,
the vacuum left where you once were
implodes my heart. Shall I endure?

Now each morning I'll look East to seek
a ray of hope that you'll be seen shining
on the footpath that leads me lonely
through the shaded grove of aging trees
and back to you, light of my life.

Wood Sprites

I remember wood sprites
in the hills where Wordsworth
walked so long before
above Lake Windemere—
saw them with my mind's eye,
for when I'd turn to catch a glimpse,
they'd tuck behind a boulder.
They took great delight
in staying out of sight
as with their impish glee
they played spy-and-hide with me,
yet I sensed their presence
as I walked along the trail.

Just so, my soul mate,
you are with me through the day
as I tread my way through wooded lanes
that overlook the lakeshore of my life.

Blessed Fog

There was a strange foreboding
in the fog that had hovered like incense,
but just now wafts off the lake,
shudders grass blades
and flutters last fall's oak leaves
as if attempting to uncover their
hoarded secrets from the past.
The fog flees ahead of the wind,
which blesses the earth
with a smattering of rain
as it whispers an "Asperges me."
A squirrel ventures out tentatively,
unsure if it is really dusk,
or merely fog-fall.
All is a wholly ghostly gray
to match my mood since you're away.

Oh, fog, wrap me in your blessed shroud
of invisibility, that none may see
the stigmata that I bear
behind the smiling masque I wear
in piercing sunshine.

Foresight

Take time along the way
to know yourself,
for loved ones die
and best friends move away.
You're really all you've got
for sure, they say.

But I'd have spent
more time with friends;
then when it's time to leave,
I'd not be cold—
wrapped in their love
there'd be no cause to grieve.

Recovery

Beachside Reverie

Scent of suntan oil drifts by
from behind the dune, which shelters
young lovers basking in the heat
of sun…and hormones.
Weary snow fence sags from wind and
unfettered explorers playing Dan'l Boone
as they conquer new territory.

We oldsters, content to sit
after conquering the drifts of sand,
arrange ourselves on bench and
prehistoric logs etched with
modern petroglyphs proclaiming,
"T C loves M J", and a phone number
to call for an emergency
good time.

A black, hairy fly in gray-striped tuxedo
buzzes urgently in circles, seeking.
He considers the phone number, lands,
pauses long enough to preen forelegs
in anticipation of a fresh morsel of scat
kept warm by the sun.

When did I grow too old
to make love behind a dune,
to forge beyond the fence,
to pledge undying love on tree trunks,
to buzz around in circles?
Has my life come to this: that I sit here
befriending the fly as it dowses my fingertip
in search of the source of my lunch?

Oh, my one, true love, are you with me here
as, dying, you had promised me?
Do you even remember my number?

Time of Your Life

Time, life's metered mentor,
plays the gracious hostess,
opening the door to more
    efficient ways,
ushering you down corridors
of seemingly infinite possibility
and into chambers furnished
    with endless potential.

Then late, as you begin
to look for her leadership
and grow dependent
    on her direction,
she disappears into a stairwell
leaving you to grope in darkness
as you find your way out
    on your own.

Medical Center Parking Lot

Shuffled steps, steadying arms, guiding hands,
leaners on four-pronged canes,
the elderly pushing walkers haltingly,
babies clutched by worried parents,
wheelchair-bound pushed by aides,
grim-faced, motorized amigo drivers,
bearded Santa sporting shorts, fatigued,
(and the toyshop season only just begun)—
these are the parking lot denizens
streaming in and out.
They hide their weary spirits
behind masks of determination.

On the adjacent highway, the incessant traffic
of the workers, the hurried, the harried,
the shoppers, the busy, stream by unaware
of the all-consuming, individual dramas
being played out on the stages
of examining tables and gurneys
behind the bleak, efficient façade
of the clinic walls.

Thank God for
    feet that carry, knees that bear up,
    courageous hearts to continue the struggle,
    eyes that can see a brighter tomorrow.

Telescape

As I lay in bed
these several days
my eyes memorized
dresser knobs,
ceiling tiles,
pictures askew
and laundry "to do".

My restless spirit
paced the room
seeking egress.
Out the open door
it floated like a moth—
barely pausing in the hall
it sought the window
on the opposite wall.
Through the glass it passed
and fluttered free
through an opening
in a leafy tree where it
gained momentum and
flew beyond the earth
into the blue opening
between the clouds.
Exuberant, it circled
a distant galaxy
on the back side
of the sky.

Bat in My Belfry

Appearing out of the dark into the half-light
as dawn trembled in the trees,
anxious to give birth to this new day,
a large bat left over from night
circled the courtyard, then bumped gently
at my window as if to say,
"Good morning, but I'm leaving now
to return to that snug space
in the crack of your chimney."
Was it sent by Camazotz, the ancient god of bats?
It seemed regal, yet light-hearted
as it signaled the coming out of darkness
into the promise of rebirth, a reminder that
it's time to die to some aspect of life
that is no longer possible.
Now must I face change, my greatest fear,
to release the old and create the new?
Its fluttering wings stir my consciousness
as yesterday's death leads to the birth of a new day,
which holds infinite possibilities.

The List

Husband gone.
Missing that companionable
conversation with a male perspective,
yet not seeking marriage,
I take the formula for the law of attraction
and draft a "list of one hundred" attributes
my ideal friend would have.

I'll never reach a hundred, I think;
but start with all the qualities
I admired in my spouse,
then add a few that I'd consider bonuses
to further enrich the relationship.
Before I know it I have one hundred and seventeen.

I don't know any one man
who possesses all these desirable traits.
Then it dawns on me:
these are the composite qualities
that are already intrinsically available
in a few of my gay acquaintances
and a horde of my women friends
who already fill my life with satisfying friendship—
proof that the law of attraction works,
sometimes retroactively!

I'm Your Man
(choose one):

Best beau,
Gigolo,
True to the end,
Good friend,
Like a brother,
Not your father,
Special someone,
Coerced companion,
All-around Great Guy,
Wonder what & wonder why,
Fantasy date,
He who waits,
Partner in fun,
Escort on the run,
Dream boat,
Pal afloat,
Good buddy,
No fuddy-duddy,
Art teacher,
Propriety preacher,
Heart-takes-wing,
Bling thing!
Main squeeze.
Eager to please.
Special friend.
The livin' end.

Commiseration

He knew my feelings all too well—
the anguish one is loathe to tell
of traveling through a personal hell.

Walking on a different path,
he suffered from a similar wrath
and bore the painful aftermath.

Be it rejection or death, whatever the bane,
whatever the cause—the result is the same:
pain is pain.

Potential

Yesterday slipped by as soundlessly as the sun
    beyond the unreachable horizon.
Now my memories fade with the sunset.
Though I trace the outlines of the past
    to keep them vivid on today's page,
they blur, then dematerialize,
    washing clear as tears flood the paper.
What shall I paint on this page
    of future possibilities?
        A bright, new painting.

Delicious Day

It's a delicious morning!
I can taste its freshness
like a juicy peach on my tongue;

but

rain could be pelting
against my picture window,
beautifully transparent like the glass
as it beads and caresses the pane,
and my pains as well;

or

a cheerful sun could be beaming
rays of happiness toward the world;

or

a storm could be brewing.

As I arise inside my snug home
I can feel the mood of this day—
its liveliness and loveliness,
its vibrancy, yet pensiveness;
and, although I'm alone, I find
myself chuckling, laughing aloud
as the joy and wonder of this day
tickle me deep down inside.

Oh, yes! It's a delicious,
delightful,
delectable day!

Another Fine Afternoon

It's another fine afternoon.
I've tiptoed past the ominous morning hours
when more people die of stroke and heart attacks,
ignored the odd, crinkly feeling in my brain
brought on by active imagination,
skulked around behind scary statistics,
tried to conquer apprehension in spite of
confusion caused by
    thinking too many things at once, and
    doing too many things at once, to avoid
    thinking of too many things at once.

    Weaving in and out of this morning
    our black-robed neighbor
    skirted the trees beyond the yard
    and padded past the window
    in her black-stockinged feet
    like a grim reaper who traded
    her scythe for a fallen oak branch.

Now it's another fine afternoon.
Was the sun shining this morning?
I hadn't noticed, but it is now.
I'm celebrating with a piece of chocolate—
rich, dark, bitter chocolate—
life is sweet enough right now:
I've won the race past the cemetery gates
and sinister morning statistics
to another fine afternoon.

Stray Dog

You limp down my lane
with a battered heart
bruised by life's cruelty.
You dig under my fence
and crawl into my yard.
With soulful eyes
you lie outside my door
hoping to be healed.

Your presence calls to me,
drawing me out to discover
the depth of your goodness.
You lie at my feet, and as you
humbly lick my own wounds,
you peel away my pretenses,
soothe my sorrow with your sighs,
reduce me to my essential elements…

and we are both healed.

Remanence

If I am ever left
with loss of strength
and health, I'll want
my mind and memories
to re-enjoy all I have done.
In my imagination
old tennis sets I'll win,
mountain peaks I'll climb,
new flowers I'll invent
and buildings I'll design
with you in mind.

In Quest

Thanks for not asking about my "-isms,"
for not squeezing me into a category;
for as a poet I am
    Christian…and Buddhist,
    cynic…and believer,
    liberal…and conservative,
    female…and male,
    critic…and lover.

I am a contradiction,
yet from my shadowed corner
    ever a seeker of light.
My sights are set on knowledge and wisdom;
    yet after the memory of learning fades,
    poetry, the language of feelings,
    will remain ever more valued;
and when I come into God's presence
    to finally see clearly
    that massive quarry of knowledge
    lying far beyond
    the great philosophers' scattered arrows,
    spent before reaching their target,
all that will matter will be
    the sense of well-being in God's presence,
        appreciation of ultimate beauty,
            and all-encompassing love.

Journey To Dawn

A white-maned horse named "Destiny"
bears me down the pavement of night.
To roar of engines and tires' whine we race
beside the comet-streaked ring of highway.
The lights recede into distant stars.

I try to urge him onto firm footing;
but his muscles tighten beneath
the leathery heat of the saddle
as he sidesteps, nostrils flaring,
then skitters and prances,
determined to chart his own course.

Veering from the road, we gallop
through fields of undefined black underbrush
and unfamiliar purple shadows
heavy with the musk of night.
Reins fly free and flow with mane and tail
to the undulation of his gait
and the rhythm of his thudding hooves.

Eyes smarting from the wind,
I peer between his pricked ears
to see what lies ahead
as his tail flicks excitedly,
shaking off the dust of a fleeting past
that I cannot hope to recapture.

Exhilarated, we speed
toward the entrance of a new dawn.

Threshold

At the unmarked exit of this world
neither gate nor door bars
entry to eternity.
The spacious aperture
through the cold, gray stone
of the physical realm
is unadorned, unrestrictive,
worn smooth by countless passages.
It is a stoma through which
life itself transpires;
and through the portal
one sees only misty darkness.

On the other side
all is mystic light
and peace.

Filtration

Like water

    straining through sand,

    our lives flow

    downward

    through time.

Grains of experience

    filter out

        our imperfections

        as we learn

            and release our mistakes

            to the past,

then ascend, purified,

    from the ultimate,

        mystical well-spring

        of rebirth.

Brevity

A punster said,
"When all is said and done,
there is usually more said than done."
So in the interest of verbal paucity
I propose that, like life, poetry
be condensed to just this:

      we live
      we laugh
      we love
      we learn
      we leave

Addendum to Acknowledgements

From my friends and mentors I've learned:

when you can't do anything else, you can still smile – Albin M.
that a good rhyme turns mere words into music – Al A.
that time with a youngster is time well-spent – Albert H.
to stand tall and keep a twinkle in your eye – Alice Y.
to keep one foot in heaven and the other on the earth – Fr. Andy B.
the meaning of self-sacrifice – Ann W. and Helen M.
to enjoy a bit of whimsy in your life – Ayun S.
that art is a transcendent spiritual activity, and I can do it – Sr. Barbara C.
that modesty is translucent; goodness shows through – Barb S.
to be an ever-acceptant and loving sister – Barb W.
to approach life with gusto and vibrancy! – Betty B.
to endure long-suffering and be willing to fly home from Florida to bake cookies with your grandchildren – Betty M.
to keep on biking, no matter what – Betty and Jim O.
to network, and have a speech ready for every occasion – Bill M.
to keep a youthful outlook, and you'll never grow old – Bill S.
to follow your creative star wherever it leads you – Bonnie L.
to dare to take charge of your life – Bonnie M.
you don't have to have children to be a good Father – Fr. Carl M.
that a loving home makes everything possible – Carl M.
that, although 3 outs end the inning, you can still win the game – Carrie M.
to seek the silver lining in God's clouded plan – Catherine K.
that energy and spirit provide the drive for accomplishment – Charlie P.
to analyze situations for cause, effect and motivation – Chris C.
to keep on keeping on and inspire others to do the same – Christine VanI.
to share your talent with others indiscriminately – Claire B-L.
to see events from a world perspective – Conchita C.
that perkiness and optimism are friend magnets – Diana L.
to use more water, take fewer strokes, and think ahead – Don B.
to be attentive, enthusiastic and interested in others – Donna E.

to be a constant, true friend and never divulge a secret – Donna Ri.
to throw yourself wholeheartedly into your art – Donna Ru.
to speak less and listen more – Doreen K.
to work hard and enjoy the results – Dottie P.
that love & acceptance are the glue between father & child – Edwin E.M.
that love gives you the strength to do what needs to be done – Ed H.M.
that calm and steady makes for good leadership and friendship – Eddie K.
that all the world's a stage, and you can be a star – Eddie M.
that pixies rule! – Ellen M.
that the greatest satisfaction comes not from your accomplishments, but in sharing your talents with others – Ernie M.
that unwavering devotion to duty provides the best example – Ervin I.
to accomplish the difficult with boundless determination – Ev H.
to think before I speak, and to be generous – Faith B.
that you don't have to BE the size of a tractor to drive one – Fran S.
to eliminate unnecessary steps in any procedure – Grace D.
that one can be ladylike, gracious and real simultaneously – Gretchen P.
that fire and ice can combine to produce interesting art – Haley M.
to just DO it, and not be afraid to take a stand – Helen W.
to do the best you can, and when you can't, a good belly laugh will make up for it – Henry G.
that gentle love kindles the twinkle in one's eyes – Hubert E. Sr.
to hold to your opinion, even if it's wrong – Hub E. Jr.
that Renaissance women have walked among us – Irene M.
to treat your talent with patience and humility – Ivoughn D.
to see the good in others and celebrate it – Jack W.
that quiet girls are lots of fun when they "come out" – Jan G.
to come through the dark night with a sparkle still in your eyes – Jennifer C.
to fly, even soar, with clipped wings – Jill M.
to keep on keeping on, no matter what – Jim M. & Mike F.
that there is life outside the city – Joanie K.
to be aware of others' needs and do something about them – Joanne B.
that brilliance is thinking and seeking, polished by education – Joe E.
if you have an impossible problem, call: 563-7249. That's – Joe Schw.
to know what's right, and do it – John U.
that a walk in the woods calms the soul & cures what ails you – Jon M.

to share your knowledge with the next generation and beyond – Judy B.
to hear the rustle of angel wings and see art in a dead stick – Judy M.
that shopping keeps your brain agile – Judy S.
to accept others without judging – Julia E.
to hostess with flair and always be gracious – Karen M.
that music makes words and hearts sing – Ken & DeeAnn G.
that needles and thread create magic in an artist's hands – Kris M.
that a potter can rise to be "Queen of Clay" – Laurie C.
to persevere through life's difficulties and still be kind – Liz W.
to be a good mother-in-love and never criticize – Lucy M.
that still waters do run deep – Lucy G.
to be flowerfully fantastic and ever in-the-know – Lynne M.
that a lively mind can take a licking and keep on ticking – Marc F.
to be an enthusiastic people-encourager – Margaret Ann R.
to flash a bit of chutzpah – Marne S.
to laugh at life's incongruities – Mary A.
to pack all you can into your days and have fun in the kitchen – Mary B.
to do your own thing, whatever others think – Maxine G.
to shine the spotlight on others even though she's a star herself – Nancy E.
to adapt, but keep standards high and goals in sight – Natalia K.
that sharing love and grief dilutes the pain – New Day Group (anon.)
to prioritize and organize – Patty F.
that devotion is demonstrated through deeds – Paul G.
when the lake is too rough to fish, tell fish stories – Phil F.
that brotherly love means you're never really separated – Ray J. M.
to look at the world in a different way – Richard W.
to think it, research it, plan it, DO it – Rich Y.
that downright goodness must come from farming the land – Ron K.
that harmless fibbing can be fun – Sam B.
to place family above all else – Sally M.
positive attitudes make life worthwhile – Scheurer LTC residents & staff
to be interested in everyone and to listen, and listen – Sharon U.
that a smile can make the sun come out – Susan McN.
the secret to staying together is to ride a tandem bike – Susan & Rick M.
to make being brilliant seem like a normal thing – Teresa M.
to approach death with dignified serenity – Theresa F.

that supporting others raises you up, too – Thumb Arts Guild members
the hardest muscles come from working hard not working out – Val S.
to play the hand you're dealt, even if you don't win – Venice F.
the best gift for a pre-teenager is your time & attention – Zeryl S.
though sometimes your name is forgotten, your deeds endure in memory.

Previously Published Poems

"Abraham Would Understand," *Impressions*, Jane Mayes, Port Austin, MI, 1993.

"Affluence Spoken Here," Honorable mention, Thumb Area Writers' Club Contest, Sandusky, MI, 1992. *A Joyful Noise*, Spiritual Pub. Co., Venice, FL, 1993. *Impressions*, 1993. *The Old Millpond Anthology*, Phil Long, ed., Big Rapids, MI, Fall 2001.

"Apple Antics," *Impressions*, 1993. *Timelapse*, a journal of poetry, Anderson, SC, Vol. 3, No. 1, Spring/Summer, 1997.

"Awareness," Honorable mention, Poetry Society of Michigan contest, 2002.

"Benevolence," Chapbook, Gaylord Council for the Arts, Gaylord, MI, 2008.

"Brass Bed," *Impressions*, 1993. *The Sweet Annie & Sweet Pea Review*, Baxter, Iowa, Vol.1, No. 2, Summer, 1996.

"Descant," Third place, "Art in the Air" poetry contest, WPON, Bloomfield Hills, MI, Dec. 1992. *Impressions*, 1993. *Passionate Hearts, the poetry of sexual love*, Wendy Maltz, ed., New World Library, Novato, CA, 1997. *Sunday Suitor*, poetry review, E. Fuller, ed., Lathrop, CA, Aug. 1997.

"Don't Go," *Seeing…Through Nature*, Jane Mayes, Author House, Bloomington, IN, 2005.

"Dream of Peace," Lyrics, music by José Maurtua, for a peace exchange to China, 2005.

"Ephemerality," *Impressions,*1993. *Women and Death*, anthology, Ground Torpedo Press, Ann Arbor, MI, 1994.

"Feral Roses," *Impressions,* 1993.

"Filtration," *Scene to Unseen,* chapbook, by Jane Mayes, Port Austin, MI, 2001. Honorable Mention, Poetry Society of Michigan contest, April, 2001. *The Port Austin Times,* July 12, 2001.

"Focus-Pocus," *Scene to Unseen,* 2001. *The Old Millpond Anthology,* Spring, 2002.

"Foresight," *Impressions,* 1993.

"Fresh Apple-Popcorn Days," *ibid.*

"Games," *Anthology,* Poetry Society of Michigan, 2006. Chapbook, Gaylord Council for the Arts, 2008.

"Gifts," *Impressions,* 1993.

"Inhumation," *Impressions,* 1993.

"Journey to Dawn," *Scene to Unseen,* 2001.

"Legal Tender," *Messages From the Heart,* Tucson, AZ, Vol. 6, Issue 3, Autumn, 1998.

"Liberation," *Seasons of the Heart,* Empress Publications, Teaneck, NJ, 1995.

"Luna Love," *Seeing...Through Nature,* 2005.

"My Hero," *Impressions,* 1993. *The Port Austin Times,* June 15, 1995. *The Sweet Annie & Sweet Pea Review,* Sweet Annie Press, Baxter, Iowa, Vol. 1, No. 1, Spring, 1996. *Lessons From Dad,* Joan Aho Ryan, ed., Health Communications, Deerfield Beach, FL, May, 1997.

"My Love Flees With the Northern Breeze," *Huron County Press,* Nov., 19, 2003. *Peninsula Poets,* Poetry Society of Michigan, October, 2003. PSM contest, third place, Humor Category, 2003.

"Mystic Mentor," Second place, Thumb Area Writers' Club contest, Sandusky, MI, 1992. *Impressions,* 1993.

"New Tricks," *Impressions,* 1993. *Lessons From Mom,* Joan Aho Ryan, ed., Health Communications, Deerfield Beach, FL, 1996. *Old Millpond Anthology,* Fall, 2001.

"Orchestration," *Passionate Hearts,* 1997.

"Path of Least Resistance," *Scene to Unseen,* 2001.

"Remanence," *Impressions,* 1993.

"Spirit of Song," Lyrics for New Century Chorale of Flint, music by Ken Galbreath, 2004.

"Summer 1941," *Impressions,* 1993.

"Telempathy," *2000: Here's to Humanity,* Shirley Richburg, ed., The People's Press, Baltimore, MD, 1999.

"The Rose," (Love's Yellow Rose) Lyrics for choral music by Ken Galbreath, 2003.

"Threshold," *Scene to Unseen,* 2001.

"To Make a Shack a Home," *Timelapse,* Anderson, SC, Fall/Winter, 1996.

"Undertow," *Impressions,* 1993.

"Weeding," *Impressions,* 1993. *Michigan Gardener,* Michigan State University, East Lansing, MI, 1993.

"What's a Mother to Do?" *Impressions,* 1993. *Lessons From Mom,* Deerfield Beach, FL, 1996.

About the Poet

Jane (Engemann) Mayes lives on the picturesque shore of Lake Huron at the tip of the "thumb" of the Michigan "mitten." Mother of three and grandmother of six, she is a retired teacher and high school librarian with a B.A. degree in French and English from Aquinas College in Grand Rapids (1956) and an M.A. in school librarianship from Central Michigan University at Mount Pleasant (1975).

Her poems have appeared in several poetry journals, anthologies and choral compositions, and have garnered some awards, most recently the Michigan Poetry Society's 2010 traveling trophy. Her newspaper column, "Lit., etc." ran for eight years in The Port Austin Times. She has written two chapbooks and a poetry collection, Seeing...Through Nature.

In addition to penning poetry and memoirs, she enjoys watercolor, pottery, biking, puddling around in her kayak, volunteering, not setting an alarm clock, walking in woods, pastures and on beaches, and being with family and friends, some of whom you meet in this book.

Life IS good!

About the Artist

An award-winning artist, Don Bullis lives between the fertile farmland of the "thumb" of Michigan and the shoreline of Lake Huron, where he is known for his colorful watercolor paintings of old, abandoned cars, locks and doorknobs, old barns and lighthouses.

His artistic ability was recognized at an early age. He attended Meinzinger School of Art before serving in the army.

Father of seven, grandfather of fourteen plus three "greats", he was a draftsman until his retirement. Since then he has had six one-man shows and taught watercolor classes in Romeo. He currently teaches classes in Troy and Port Austin. His work may be seen at art shows in Eastern Lower Michigan and at his gallery on Grindstone Road east of Port Austin.

A past president of the Thumb Area Artists of Romeo, he is past president and current board member of the Thumb Arts Guild, and one of the Bards of Bird Creek. In his travels he enjoys seeking out covered bridges and old mills to paint. To view a sample of his work, go to thumbartsguild.com/artists.

Come along as the poet takes you on a road trip through life with its poignant, commonplace and absurd moments captured by her pen as she observes people along the route. You might even recognize yourself as you travel through the book.
Enjoy the ride!